COMMENDATIONS
for
SPIRITUAL STEPS ON THE ROAD TO SUCCESS

"I absolutely love this book. Far from being the expected How-to, or To-do kind of book, Linda gives us an incredible, fascinating read. She has taken a unique and simple, yet profound, look at her life and the lives of those who are successful. This is a provocative, honest portrayal of success as a journey, not only from a cultural, but from a faith perspective.

"What greater question can a serious person ask than, 'Who am I and what is the meaning of my life?' And what greater success is there than to find the answer to that question? In her journey and search, Linda has discovered the answer."

— *Yvonne Lehman,*
award-winning, best-selling author of 47 books, founder and director of
Blue Ridge Mountains Christian Writers Conference

* * *

"Brilliant, evocative; easy to read, and very inspiring."
— *Dr. Douglas E. Millham,*
President, Discover the World, Inc

* * *

"For me, one of the great values of the book is the emphasis and exploration of integrity in our professional lives – everyone talks about excellence and commercial instincts, no one talks about the marks of integrity, and how to put a grid up to measure your progress with a biblical worldview. Too many people don't know how to define success or what they want out of life. Thank you for the milestones you have pointed out, no matter where you are in the journey, for determining our progress and our orientation to true north."

— *Ralph Winter,*
Executive Producer, X-Men *and* Lost

* * *

"Sometimes the best personal therapy is to boost your energy and clarity by reading a few chapters of a highly-inspiring book. Dr. Linda Seger's excellent and easy-to-read *Spiritual Steps on the Road to Success* is insightful, profound, and very practical. It will help a lot of good souls to do great things in the world while staying balanced in their personal lives."

– *Leonard Felder, PhD,*
author of Fitting in is Overrated

* * *

"Linda Seger has more than twenty years' experience working in the top echelons of the Hollywood film industry. Her insights and wisdom have helped propel an entire generation of screenwriters and producers to a higher level of quality. In her latest book, Seger offers a unique assessment of what it means to be successful without compromising one's faith. The pitfalls, the hazards, the essential questions that each of us need to answer - all are covered in a smooth and easy-to-read fashion. Highly recommended."

– *Davis Bunn,*
bestselling author

* * *

"Some of the best spiritual writing since C.S. Lewis. This book is essential reading for young graduates as they respond to the dual challenges of their professional and spiritual lives. The book contains fascinating interviews from seasoned professionals who have travelled the career path and have profound spiritual wisdom to share, as does Linda herself.

"I shall insist that all my film and television graduates read it. My only regret is that such a book did not exist when I started out on my own career in the media; had I read it I might have avoided some of the spiritual pitfalls."

- *Andrew Quicke,*
Professor of Cinema-Television, Regent University

* * *

"Linda's book confirms the truth of my favorite quote by Miles Davis, who said, 'It takes a long time to learn how to play like yourself.' Giving profound insights, this book wisely outlines the spiritual steps every artist, entrepreneur, or desperate housewife must take to find our own voice or calling, in order to fulfil our life's purpose and become who God created us to be - which is the road to success!"

– James Covell,
composer and author

* * *

"This is an important book that fills a much-needed niche in the spiritual literature, grounded as it is in the everyday work situations of a very wide variety of people. Starting from secular contexts, it seeks to demonstrate how people of faith make sense of their lives and their role in the world. As a result, the damaging boundaries so often encountered between the worlds of faith and of work are nowhere to be found.

"While Linda Seger's writing is unreservedly contemporary, her reliance on biblical teaching is evident throughout. What is so refreshing is that there is never a hint of any slipshod, packaged or superficial answers. She is always prepared to stand up to the demands and sometimes tragedies of everyday existence.

"Of the numerous gems in the book a number caught my attention. The chapter on 'being important' is particularly insightful. How often does one encounter the issues that arise when you become a public person, when everyone wants a piece of you, and when you become the object of resentment?

"The analysis of the seven deadly sins is masterly, rescuing them from the historical obscurity that so often characterizes their treatment. The discussion of envy, covetousness, lust and gluttony, for instance, is exceedingly practical and very down-to-earth, with illustrations of what these sins mean in the contemporary world of work. Their relevance for today shines through with breath-taking clarity."

- D Gareth Jones,
Professor of Anatomy and Structural Biology, University of Otago,
New Zealand

* * *

"Dr. Seger explores this topic from a spiritual perspective that is both deeply Christian and refreshingly universal. Trained in theology as well as in theater, she is at home in the world of Hollywood as well as in a broad range of religious communities, from the born-again conservative Christian to the pacifist progressive Quaker. She examines both the opportunities and the pitfalls of success, and gives useful advice on how to stay centered in the face of hard choices and career challenges. I highly recommend it for anyone setting out on a new career, or contemplating a career change."

- Dr. Anthony Manousos,
Quaker author, and editor of EarthLight

* * *

"This is an incredible work, a veritable how-to book for Christians. Linda Seger, a Hollywood insider, has spent years learning lessons from her personal and professional life, and takes us on a journey to explain the 'how to' for those who want to be sure that God is in the center of their business life. She has sprinkled the book with quotations from the Bible, from great philosophers and writers, as well as waitresses, parents, children, academics and filmmakers, and is as likely to quote scripture as a line from a well known feature film.

"This book is a must for all to read, no matter what your religious conviction, and will provide a road map to living in the footsteps of Jesus Christ."

– Larry Mortorff,
executive producer of Billy, The Preacher *and* Oscar Romero

* * *

Dr. Linda Seger has three MAs and a ThD in the fields of drama and theology. Author of ten books, she has consulted on over 2000 scripts including more than forty produced feature films and thirty-five produced television projects. She is in demand as a speaker and seminar leader and has taught in more than thirty countries.

SPIRITUAL
STEPS ON THE ROAD TO
SUCCESS

Gaining the goal without losing your soul

Linda Seger, ThD

MONARCH
BOOKS

Oxford, UK & Grand Rapids, Michigan, USA

Published in association with Benrey Literary, www.benreyliterary.com

First published in the UK in 2009 by Monarch Books
(a publishing imprint of Lion Hudson plc),
Wilkinson House, Jordan Hill Road, Oxford OX2 8DR.
Tel: +44 (0)1865 302750 Fax: +44 (0)1865 302757
Email: monarch@lionhudson.com
www.lionhudson.com

ISBN: 978-1-85424-888-6 (UK)
ISBN: 978-0-8254- 6294-8 (USA)

Distributed by:
UK: Marston Book Services Ltd, PO Box 269, Abingdon, Oxon OX14 4YN;
USA: Kregel Publications, PO Box 2607, Grand Rapids, Michigan 49501

Unless otherwise stated, Scripture quotations are taken from the Holy Bible, New International Version, © 1973, 1978, 1984 by the International Bible Society. Used by permission of Hodder & Stoughton Ltd. All rights reserved.

This book has been printed on paper and board independently certified as having come from sustainable forests.

British Library Cataloguing Data
A catalogue record for this book is available from the British Library.

Printed and bound in England by CPI Cox & Wyman.

Dedicated to my cousins:

Pauline Sateren from the Seger side of my family – music educator, church musician, soprano soloist. Her professionalism, grace, openness and good humor have been models for me throughout my adult life.

and

Rev. Brooks Graebner, from the Graebner side of my family – Rector at St. Matthew's Episcopal Church in Hillsborough, North Carolina, whose intellect, compassion, graciousness and kindness have been a light to me since I was eight years old.

CONTENTS

ACKNOWLEDGMENTS

With many thanks to my editor, Tony Collins, who has made the writing of this book such a great joy; and to my agent, Janet Benrey, whose strategizing and support make writing such a pleasure.

Many thanks to my readers, who provided insight, questions, ideas, and constant support: Cathleen Loeser, Elona Malterre, Lori Marett, Kim Peterson, Pamela Jaye Smith, and Devorah Cutler Rubenstein.

And to other readers who gave me additional feedback on various chapters: Steve Berendt, Eric David, and Jana Rutledge.

To the many people who recommended other people to me: DiAnn Mills, Sherah and Emma Jean Thompson Ted Baehr and Karen and Jim Covell from the United States, Simon Dooley and John Hackwell from Australia, and to all those who dropped hints, gave me suggestions, and cheered me on.

To my assistant, Sarah Callbeck, who keeps so many things in my office organized and clear.

And always to my husband, Peter Le Var, who was a sounding-board, a cheerleader, and is the constant love in my life.

Foreword

On the shelves of any major bookseller you will find dozens of books about success. The ABC's of it, the secret of it, the seven, ten, or twelve steps to it, the loser's guide and the winner's guide to grabbing the brass ring before the ride is over. There are even books that discuss spiritual and religious elements of achieving success. But so far, I have found nothing quite as exciting and practical as Linda Seger's encouraging, intelligent take on the subject. Perhaps it is because for years she has been intimately acquainted with so many successful and unsuccessful, spirit-filled and spiritually-bereft professionals in arguably the most success-driven industry in the world, the entertainment business. It is a world where the stakes are so high, the egos so large, and the consequences so devastating that I have often wondered how anyone can survive show business without a strong spiritual foundation to sustain them. And yet, it's been my experience that most not only achieve success without taking spiritual steps on the road to success, they have survived the trip while actively rejecting a spiritual life.

But is survival enough?

As far as I know, no one has ever been dragged kicking and screaming down the road to success. Success is a choice. You may be pushed onto the road by family pressure, peer pressure, financial or cultural pressure. You may embark on the journey out of a sense of duty or even guilt. But those who travel the road, stay on the road and survive to reach the end of it succeed because they want it. They really want it. Usually more than anything else in life.

Sometimes the desire to succeed is so great that important questions never get answered before we fling ourselves onto the road. Questions such as, "Do I really have what it takes?", "What am I willing to sacrifice to get there?", and, of course, the big question at the start of every journey, "How do I get there and what should I pack?"

The road to success is like any other trip: we have to pack for it. And, like most trips, we don't realize what we forgot to bring along until we find ourselves really needing the one thing we left behind because we assumed it would just weigh us down, slow us up, or wouldn't be missed.

I love to pack. From my mother, a frequent flier, I learned how to pack three weeks of clothing and accessories into two carry-on bags. Granted, those bags weighed a hundred pounds, but in a pinch, I never saw my mother lacking for a towel, a hair dryer, a rain hat, an AC adapter or even a portable clothesline. I'll never forget her expression of joyful victory when she once produced a small hot pot and two envelopes of soup from her shoulder bag during an unexpected layover in the Dallas/Ft. Worth airport. She negotiated airports the way generals survey and attack a battle field. With Mother, travel was an art to be perfected. "Always use carry-on, sit on the aisle for quick getaways, keep smiling at the ticket agent, and if your flight is cancelled, don't follow the crowd, go to the nearest phone booth and book your own ticket while the others are waiting in line. Above all, keep moving forward and trust that whatever you might need, you are already carrying with you." Her advice for those cross country trips resulted in not just easier travel, but gave me a tremendous sense of confidence and autonomy as I began exploring the world on my own. While I discovered that much of her practical wisdom – moving forward, packing for the rainy day, etc. – could apply to the pursuit of my dreams as well as to travel, I learned that there is one big difference between a flight across the country and journey toward success. It is knowing how to pack for the longer, more difficult trip toward success. Because when you get to the end of that road, you may not be the same person you were when you left home.

Near the end of the movie *Almost Famous* there is a scene, perhaps the definitive cinematic moment in the film, that may also be the definitive illustration of the road to success. Cameron Crowe, a man who knows Hollywood well and the human spirit even better, wrote and directed a story about an aspiring rock and roll critic, a teenage boy whose dream comes true when he manages to land an assignment from *Rolling Stone* magazine to go on the road with Stillwater, an up-and-coming rock band on the edge of greatness.

The wide-eyed neophyte follows the lives and loves of the aspiring rock stars as they make the transition from small venues to large, from the middle of the charts to the top, from bus tours to private jets. Finally, with the help of their teenage chronicler, they capture the ultimate flag of success: the cover of *Rolling Stone*.

Almost immediately, on one of those private jets, everything they've worked for, everything everyone on that plane has dreamed of is nearly lost. In one terrifying moment, their smooth sailing deteriorates into turbulence, lightning strikes, and heart-clutching plunges toward earth as the pilots attempt an emergency landing.

Between screams of terror, the coolest and the hippest shrivel before our eyes into frightened children crying out embarrassing confessions and hurling accusations at one another. In their darkest hour, friendship and loyalties are forgotten, the romance of the road becomes sinister, and the possibility of a mythic Buddy Holly brand of immortality is now far less attractive than a hard, ignominious landing in a farmer's field. Not one calls out to a higher power, not one finds hope or strength in the sex, drugs, and rock and roll that brought them to his moment. In fact, in the two or three minutes when death seems certain, success is not only forgotten, it is useless.

They survive. But the band and the teenage boy who witnessed the rise and fall of his heroes emerge from the plane very different people, unable to look at each other, soberly lost in thought and in shame. They know now that they could just have easily ended up in *Rolling Stone* as an obituary instead of a cover story, and life would have gone on without them. And yet, with some embarrassment, they sense they have been a given a second chance despite the fact that they miserably failed a crucial test of character on the road to success. With all the luggage and baggage they carried from gig to gig, their "spiritual suitcase" never made it on the trip.

Almost Famous is fiction and provides a tremendously satisfying ending where the main characters recognize their chance of redemption and take it. On the real life road, though, we don't always get those chances before the credits roll. Or, when we do, it sometimes just seems too far or too late to go back and retrieve the spiritual map we forgot or simply decided not to pack. But with every decision to leave matters of the spirit behind, there are consequences.

. Bible readers and non-Bible readers alike are familiar with the Scripture, "What good is it for a man to gain the whole world, yet forfeit his soul?" Few of us embark on the journey toward success actually believing that this warning might actually apply to *us*. *Others* may be tempted to compromise their integrity or their vision; *others* may justify the means by exalting the end, but I won't, right?

I would like to think that I avoided compromise and temptation more than most during the successful years of *Touched By An Angel*. But truth be told, every day was a struggle for survival professionally and sometimes even literally when my energy and health took a back seat to the demands of keeping a weekly television hit in the Top Ten. I certainly wasn't dragged kicking and screaming onto the road to success, but I was running hard to catch up and frantically packing my spiritual bag as I ran. I am proud of most of my days and decisions on that show. Of some days, particularly the early days when the learning curve was steep and my spiritual resources were shallow, I am not so proud. In some of Linda's observations in this book, I see myself and my mistakes. And yet, in other pages, I recognize my subsequent growth and hard-earned wisdom, achieved not so much by my victories but by my submission and reliance on God's grace. And most importantly, years after the trappings of worldly success have subsided – the awards, the magazine covers, the private planes, the accolades – I see confirmed in Linda's book my own discovery that there is a life after success and a purpose beyond that success which brings a peace even greater than the temporary goal I had originally struggled to reach.

Wisely, kindly, with her gentle sense of Quaker simplicity and fairness, Linda reminds us of the true nature of success and the role that spirituality can play in turning the brass ring into a golden key. If there is a secret to success at all, it is that success is not the end of the road; it's a door. It is the entrance to a world where power, money, and sometimes fame are simply tools we've been given to create something beyond ourselves and our accomplishments. True success is not the private plane that takes us away from it all. It is the crash landing that puts us squarely back in the middle of it, packed and ready to make a difference.

It all comes down to what you choose to carry with you and what you decide to leave behind on the trip. As you will find in the pages that follow, it is never too late to re-pack that bag. And whether you are dreaming of success, actively pursuing it, or have already achieved some measure of it; Linda Seger has written the best packing list I have ever read.

Martha Williamson
Pasadena, California 2009

Introduction

Again I tell you, it is easier for a camel to go through the eye of a needle than for a rich man to enter the kingdom of God.

Matthew 19:24

What good is it for a man to gain the whole world, yet forfeit his soul?

Mark 8:36

Life is a spiritual test. This is true, not just for the bad, but also for the good. We might tend to think that all the spiritual issues we confront relate to the negatives in our lives – such as addiction, abuse, illness, unemployment, break-ups, and the death of a loved one. But achieving our goals, being successful, being famous, well respected, and even rich, also present us with spiritual challenges, and they are often spiritual issues that are easy to ignore because of the comfort and respect that we have and the good life that we have achieved. We all know people who have blown it – no matter what the circumstances. And we all know people who have handled their success well and used it to manifest the Kingdom among us.

We live and work in the world, yet we often feel a tension between doing well and doing good, between being successful in the world's terms and maintaining integrity in our spiritual lives, knowing that sometimes they may demand opposite actions. We try to hear the still, small voice that calls us, but it can be muted by our desire to accomplish and achieve on our terms.

For those of us working publicly in the world – in careers that have the potential to influence others as well as impact the world – our ability to pass the test and to be an instrument and partner with God becomes ever more important. Our commitment to actualizing the values of justice, compassion, tolerance, kindness, and goodness can have enormous influence on our happiness, our relationships with others, and our world.

All of us, of course, can do good in the world – whether we're spiritual or not. But if you're a person actively working to bring the Spirit into your life, and if you're a person who wants to do work which you feel God wants you to do, and to express God's goodness through your work, new questions and challenges arise.

That is what this book explores – the spiritual challenges we meet when we want God in the center of our professional lives. The book explores the temptations, the resistances, the obstacles that try to keep us from getting through the eye of the needle. It explores processes we can use to move us from one step to another.

The book is divided into three parts, since the steps we take seem to fall into either the beginning, when we start on the journey, the middle, when we're well on our way and meet a number of obstacles, and toward the end, when we are achieving our dream or have achieved it and find there are whole new issues to address when we've finally made it. Although each person might meet some of these issues in a slightly different order than are mentioned in this book, and there may be one or two you won't meet at all, chances are, you will have some interaction with each of those mentioned.

The book is written from a Christian perspective,

but I hope that non-Christians will find that many of the universal spiritual ideas in this book will resonate with them as well.

I write from a fairly broad religious background. I'm the granddaughter of a Lutheran minister with a family tree of numerous ministers, missionaries, and theologians who run the gamut from fundamentalist Christians to liberal Christians to no religion at all. Some of my great-great grandparents and grand-uncles migrated to Australia in the early 1900s and became influential in the Lutheran Church and Lutheran Seminary there.

When I was twenty-one, I became a born-again Christian and made a commitment to try to put God in the center of my life. In 1970, I became a Quaker (that is, a member of the Society of Friends) and in 1971, I decided to study theology in a seminary in Berkeley which consisted of a consortium of nine different seminaries. I took classes from the Baptists and Methodists and Lutherans and Catholics and Episcopalians and Presbyterians, and focused on classes in Theology and the Arts. I received an MA in Religion and the Arts from Pacific School of Religion and a ThD in Drama and Theology from the Graduate Theological Union.

In the 1990s, I was lonesome for the academic study of theology and decided to return to school. I attended a Catholic graduate school – Immaculate Heart College Center in Los Angeles – and received an MA in Feminist Spirituality in 2000.

My work life has focused on drama – first as a college professor in theater, and since 1979, in the film industry. I created my job in 1981 as a script consultant and script troubleshooter, based on my doctoral dissertation that developed a method for understanding why a script (for film, television, and theater) worked, or didn't work. The creation of the job took a huge leap of faith for me, since this job didn't exist and no one was used to paying for feedback on their scripts except in the few screenwriting classes that existed in the early 1980s.

I felt called to drama since the age of nineteen, and through many years, the exact calling began to be worked out. I determined, at the beginning of my consulting career, to try to apply spiritual principles to my work even when I wasn't sure what they were. I wanted my work to have integrity, and to be Spirit-filled, and over the years, I began to understand what some of those principles were. Most of the principles discussed in this book I've learned from my own experience.

Throughout the book, you will hear voices, other than mine, talk about their experience and their faith and how they practise it within their work. A few of their names will be well known to you. Many will not, although many are well known within their own field which spans the arts and sciences and business and social sciences. I tried to find Christians who came from many walks of life, from different denominations, and from many different places in the world. I interviewed people from many countries – including Great Britain and Africa, the United States and India, New Zealand, Australia and Singapore. I interviewed Baptists and Episcopalians and Lutherans and Quakers and Brethren and Presbyterians and Catholics, among many others. But I was not just looking for famous people. I wanted to find people who may not be as well known, but are living out their faith and making a difference in the world. I talked to several people within my home town of Colorado Springs, in hopes of encouraging you to discuss some of these issues with people from your own home town as well. You will find questions at the end of each chapter for discussion, which could be used in a Book Club or church discussion group or with friends. Hopefully you will find the ideas provocative and worth your reflection.

When choosing people to interview, I looked for people who were successful within their own work and who seemed to have a vibrant faith that guided them. I defined success not by money and fame, but by whether the person felt they had been called, pulled, shoved, nudged, or led into their profession and were doing work that expressed their spirituality in some way, whether through medicine or art or science or social service. I sought out people who were making a living at what they were doing and thereby were able to continue to do it. And I tried to find people who were good at what they did and respected for it. Many people came to me through recommendations of others. Some I sought out, because I had heard of them. Some I already knew and respected, and had heard them say something in normal conversation that caught my attention. Writing this book deepened my thinking about the many issues that revolve around success, and blessed me in these interactions with others.

Although the book is written from a God-centered perspective, I also understand that people use many names for God. At times, I will be speaking about the Spirit, or the Presence. You might address God as Lord, Holy Father, or Holy One. There are also certain Bible verses that point to the feminine attributes of God,[1] or as the Creator, Compassionate One, Guide, Comforter, Providence or that Power greater than ourselves.

As a Quaker, I tend to see myself as a bridge between

people from different spiritual disciplines. Quakers, as a whole, tend to believe that ours is not the only spiritual path, but a spiritual path that some of us find suits our specific needs and yearnings and seekings. As a result, we tend to be encouraging of however others choose to nurture the Spirit within. We call this Spirit by many names: the Seed, the Light Within, the Christ Within, the Indwelling God or Spirit. We believe this Spirit is constantly present, it's personal, and it can guide us, no matter the circumstance.

You will notice that the book raises questions and discusses some answers. It invites you to reflect on how you interact with these issues. Life is a mystery and not everything has clear-cut answers that can be handed to any of us. I believe in the ongoing dialogue with God as we try to work out what we're doing, why we're doing it, and how to keep spiritually balanced in the process.

I hope, in this book, to talk about the intersection of our spiritual lives and our professional lives in ways that will help you examine spiritual issues from whatever your spiritual viewpoint or whatever your denomination. I hope this book helps you explore some ideas and insights that can support your spiritual journeys. I believe that God loves us, desires to nurture our abilities, and calls us to make a difference in our world. I believe that no matter where you are in your spiritual life, and which spiritual practice you're a part of, you will resonate with the issues discussed. I hope all readers will find this book opens up new possibilities for faith and practice, as we all continue to deepen our relationship with the Spirit that transforms our work.

Part 1

Beginning the Journey

CHAPTER 1

Who Am I? Where Am I Called?

all of us … have observed frequent instances of a superintending providence in our favor … have we now forgotten that powerful Friend? Or do we imagine we no longer need his assistance?

Benjamin Franklin (Constitutional Convention, 1787)

There are two essential questions that everyone who wants to have a successful life asks, in one form or another: "Who am I?" and "What is the meaning of my life?" If we get the answer to these questions wrong, we get our life wrong. The consequences of not coming to terms with these questions can include disappointment, the waste of our talents, anxiety, uncertainty, fear, resentment, anger, or even giving up. If we don't feel as if we're doing God's will in some way in our life's work, we may miss out on the depth of life and the fullness of our relationship to God. The potential for joy and influence in our work can be diminished.

Happy and successful people have many ways of articulating what it means to have a good life. Some say their life works, that it's functional. They feel content. They feel on track.

Some say their life flows. They have no resistance or conflict between what they want and what they have.

They aren't yearning for something that is somewhere out there, beyond their reach.

Some say they feel as if they are doing what they're called to do. It's as if our greatest skills and our intrinsic talents have merged with God's desire and need for us. We are aligned with Something, or Someone, beyond ourselves that seems to know, intrinsically, who and what we are, what we can become, and what we're asked to contribute. We are suited to what we do. Our careers and our identity are a good fit.

For many of us who are spiritual, it's not enough to do our job well, to enjoy it, to be respected for what we do, and to make a living doing it. We are looking to match our understanding of our identity with our Creator's call to be who we are meant to be.

Who am I?

You may have noticed how often the question of identity comes up for us. Psychologists ask identity questions if we're in therapy: "Who are you?" "How do you define yourself apart from the definitions given to you by your parents, your culture, your school, your religion, and the many pressures that try to make us different than who we really are?"

Novels and films and plays explore identity through stories. In many stories, the main characters might not know who they are, or what they're capable of, and discover it throughout the film – whether it's Rocky or Frodo or Erin Brockovich. Some stories deal with a character who must change his or her identity in some way, and we watch the film and read the story to see if the character will be able to fit into the new mold (such as King Arthur, the Karate Kid, the characters in *The Matrix*) or will return to the stable but less fulfilling life that he or she once had (such as Viola in *Shakespeare in Love* or the characters in *Sideways* or *Bridges of Madison County*). Many times, characters get hooked into the wrong identity and can't get unhooked (*Sunset Boulevard, Crash, Leaving Las Vegas*). Other times, after a long struggle, characters achieve what they've always wanted to do (*My Brilliant Career, Mr. Holland's Opus, Rocky, Apollo 13*).

In real life, we just have to read the newspapers to see how many people, even those who are wealthy and powerful, seem to have unsuccessful lives. We might say they don't fully know who they are. From Howard Hughes to Milkin the Junk Bond King to Ken Lay, whose mismanagement led to the destruction of Enron, to Leona Helmsley, the wealthy head of the Helmsley hotels who landed in jail, later died, and willed her millions to her dog – we can see that worldly success does not always lead to a fulfilled and authentic life.

Spiritual teachers from every religion suggest we recognize that our identity includes more than this physical world. They try to introduce us to the spiritual world – to define it and encourage us to enter fully into it. In fact, they tell us our very lives are at stake – if we miss this part of our identity.

Look to our childhood

The poet, William Wordsworth, writes that we come into this world, "trailing clouds of glory." In his poem, *Intimations of Childhood*, he says that somehow we are very close to God when we are born. We immediately know what's important in life – love, relationship, trust, care, sensitivity. For many children, they retain that understanding for several years. Their favorite childhood books tell them the truth about life. *The Velveteen Rabbit* tells them that they have to be real, and that sometimes becoming and being real will mean some tatters and hard knocks along the way. *Charlotte's Web* tells them that they are Quite Something, and deserving of a good life. *The Little Prince* tells them that the meaning of life is not about the expensive big house and that they mustn't get lost and confused along the way.

But most of us eventually lose our way. We get caught up in the things of the world. We learn to live by getting and spending. By the time we start our careers, we often have forgotten what's important and leave the dream and the beauty behind.

Yet, our childhood tells us something about who we are and who we're meant to be. Our defining of ourselves takes place from an early age – when we learn whether we love science or the arts, whether we're a people-person or like to go it alone, whether we fit neatly into our family's and school's expectations, or rebel against what we're told we're supposed to think and do.

We often can discover our true identity by looking back to what we naturally loved as children. My husband has a theory (which I also believe) that we can best find out what we're meant to do when we grow up by looking at what we loved to do when we were young. Our childhood joys give us a good clue about who we truly are.

As a boy, my husband loved to massage his grandmother's feet and hands, and he became a massage therapist.

My career consultant said her mother used to ask her for advice, even when she was five. And she happily gave it. She's been a career consultant for more than twenty-five years.

When I learned to talk, I didn't want to stop. I loved to talk and talk. My sister often said to my mother, "Linda has been talking for the last three hours." My mother would answer, "She has something to say!" When I was ten, I learned a new way to talk – through writing stories. When I grew up, I became a public speaker and seminar leader and author. Now I can give seminars and talk for up to eight hours at a time and write hundreds of pages about the things I love to talk about.

We sometimes think our identity is determined solely by our talents. Of course, we have to have some talent for what we do, or we won't enjoy doing it. But talent often develops. The idea that we're somehow born with all sorts of abilities that determine our careers is only partially true. Yes, most of the great singers had good voices when young. But other successful people, such as Albert Einstein and the artist Grandma Moses were slow starters and late bloomers and didn't quite fit into the mold.

We live in an in-between world. It's as if we come from God, trailing those clouds of glory, and then spend our lives trying to re-find how God's presence and influence and love works within our lives. Something may be pulling at us, but we aren't always sure quite what it is. Finding what we're meant to do and be isn't always so easy and clear.

The Quaker theologian and activist Elise Boulding says, "That which we are born remembering ... is not a 'how to'. It is God as presence. All of prayer, all of meditation, seeks that from which we came, that toward which we move."[2]

We are constantly in the process of becoming more fully ourselves and bringing God's Spirit and Guiding Presence more completely into our lives. It's as if we have to remember who we are, because, somewhere along the way, we forgot it. Most of us, as we grow up, want to bring our understanding into the work we do. We try to match our identity with our skills and with our careers, hoping to contribute something that is truly our own, and that is truly God's desire.

Yet, there are always pressures and influences that try to make us someone else. Our parents want us to follow in their footsteps. Our teachers want us to do what they do – and often in the same way they do it. Our spouses, co-workers, bosses, and even our society have an opinion about what's an appropriate career for us. The media and our culture try to tell us what are the best choices for a successful life. Meanwhile, we keep wondering, "What am I supposed to be doing? What am I best suited for?" And if we're spiritual people, we ask another question: "What does God want of me? What would success mean, from a spiritual viewpoint?"

Who are we, really?

In the 1950s, one of the most popular shows on television was *The Loretta Young Show*. Loretta Young had been an Academy Award-winning actress in feature films, but decided to enter the new world of television because she wanted to make a difference, particularly as an inspiration to girls and young women. She described herself as a "rip-roaring Catholic" and sometimes got into trouble with her sponsors for bringing too much religious content into her shows.[3] At the beginning of every show she would enter a lovely living-room, dressed to the nines in the most elegant clothes, and tell the audience something about the meaning of the story they were about to see, or she would enter at the end, telling the audience about the meaning of what they had just seen.

I was a great fan of the show, and even years later, was able to remember a number of episodes. One episode was about an interviewer who decided to ask the question, "Who are you?" of a series of people. The characters who answered defined themselves in many ways – in terms of wealth or position or their role in life. One man answered in terms of his new identity: "I'm getting a divorce." At the end, the interviewer (played by Loretta Young) thought about all the answers and realized that no one answered about their true identity: "I am a child of God."

To get to the core of who we are – as a child of God – we sometimes have to strip away all our other roles that have been handed to us, or that we've accepted without much thought – whether of mother, daughter, son, father, home-owner, head of a business, churchgoer or non-churchgoer, atheist or believer – to find what is truly essential and then build up a more authentic identity. This becomes important because all other identities can be taken away from us, and can leave us bereft, unless we understand that, at our most essential core, we belong to God, not to ourselves.

What happens to our identity when we realize we are loved, and beloved, by our Creator? However you define God, there is a connection between us and Something or Someone greater than we are. Whether it's that small inner voice that guides us and nurtures us into who we are meant to be, or a sense of something transcendent and sacred that pulls us into our identity, from our first to our last breath we are loved into being.

For the spiritual person, the Who-We-Are is rarely seen in the world's terms. We have bigger issues to deal with than owning the red Porsche and the mansion and the stocks and bonds. In spite of the pull to wealth and power, that is not what we're about. If wealth and clout is a by-product of our work, it's probably fine with us, but it isn't the essential core of what we seek.

What do we want? What calls us? To find the answer, we need to push aside the world's issues of fame and fortune to see clearly. If we listen to the authentic voice that seems to know who we are, and calls us to become that person, then we will find a few basic issues that are part of our true identity.

Our first answer will be: "It's not about materialism." Anything material is a by-product of our true identities. Some say we are physical beings in a spiritual body and some say we are spiritual beings in a physical body, but however you define it, you are talking about a sense that it is the spiritual world that we serve and that determines what we are and what we can be.

What is this thing we call success?

When we hear the word "success", many of us immediately think of how the world defines success – by wealth, by power, by position, by fame, by prominence

31

in our field, by the respect that others give us. For some people, success depends on how much kowtowing everyone is doing to them, and whether they have the clout to get the best of everything – the best seat on the plane and in the theater, the best food and wine, the trophy spouse and the envy of everyone else.

Some think of success as the prosperity gospel which believes that we are meant to be prosperous, even wealthy, and if we only pray enough, good things will come our way. If they don't, well, there must be something wrong with us and with our prayers.

But in my view, these definitions have little to do with a spiritual viewpoint about success. Most spiritual people would find the above definitions to be superficial and ultimately empty. Yes, sometimes the abundant life mentioned in the Bible includes wealth and fame and respect, but not always.

In fact, spiritual success doesn't always neatly fit into any of these categories and may actually contradict these definitions.

British physicist Wilson Poon realizes that even the word "success" does not always sit easily with spirituality. He says, "A wandering Palestinian rabbi put up for the death penalty by his own people and crucified by the Romans as a malefactor hardly counts as a 'success'. True, Christ is raised from the dead, and we have new life in him. But Paul, writing to the Colossians, says that our new life is hidden with God in Christ. And he reminded the Corinthians that not many of them were among the 'successful' of society."

Obviously, we have to think differently about what success truly is.

I asked a number of Christians how they would

define success. Although the answers had much in common with each other, each answer seemed to add another element to the definition.

Comedian Torry Martin, who performs throughout the United States, says: "For most people success is simply completing anything they intended. True success though is doing what God intends you to do and allowing him to complete you." For Torry, success adds to us as well as adding to God's work in our world. Our work brings us closer to God. We become better and more complete people in the process of succeeding at the task. Completion and going through the process of perfection is part of spiritual success.

Dr. Andrew Gosler is a scientist from the Edward Grey Institute in the Department of Zoology at Oxford. Gosler says: "As a Christian, success is more to do with the real value of one's research, i.e., the impact it makes in the real world." Andrew defines success partly in terms of doing good in the world. For him, this good includes "reducing biodiversity loss, reducing suffering, injustice and poverty."

Another scientist, Dr. D. Gareth Jones, Professor in Anatomy and Structural Biology at the University of Otago in New Zealand, says, for the scientist, "Success is measured far more in terms of riddles answered or favorite ideas overturned, than of positions occupied or money earned. I am, of course, aware that this is a far purer approach than is sometimes the case, since the power emanating from being the first to discover something or find a cure for some illness is frequently a major driving force. Indeed, the names that immediately spring to mind in any branch of science tend to be of those who have been the first to describe a phenomenon or elucidate a theory that has stood the test of time. And yet success for most scientists is far less obvious than this. It is the intellectual satisfaction of having made an advance, of having pushed forward the boundaries of knowledge, regardless of whether this is in a fundamental area of science or a highly applied area.

"Success, therefore, can seem to be strikingly self-indulgent, but it is a reflection of what we are as creative beings. Understanding how the world works is what is crucial, whether this be at the level of the human body as a whole, or of an organ like the brain, or of the digestive or respiratory system, at the cellular level, or down to the molecular level; it makes no difference. All levels of explanation are important."

Gareth sees success as helping others: "No matter where one is in science, one's actions have repercussions at many levels. For me, this element of servanthood has always been crucial, although it is an element that has to be imposed upon one's activities. However, this is hardly confined to the scientific and academic arena. But constant reminders are required emphasizing that this is what lies at the heart of spiritual success."

Dr. Douglas E. Millham is the President of Discover the World, Inc., and oversees several humanitarian programs in Kenya. Douglas warns about the dangers of success, and the way that ego can overcome our work. This is true not just for the secularist, but also for those who work in the social services and particularly for Christians: "We leaders, world changers, social engineers, and Christian entrepreneurs don't really confront spiritual issues when we become successful and effective … we avoid them. Until they confront us. We're too busy saving the world, rescuing a continent, fixing a nation, to often reflect upon how neo-colonial we are becoming, or how self-worshipping, to be brutally honest. There is a heady power that must be constantly and consciously released or it will hold anyone captive. In fact, the use (and abuse) of power among the poor can be an addictive drug for many in leadership, just as it is in any for-profit organization. I might substitute the world 'obedience' for success, and effectiveness, and efficiency. Success is the wrong term, borrowed from the wrong professions. But if you push me to define 'success', I'd say 'one child at a time, inspired and empowered to believe she can grow up into a safe future with opportunity and hope or one group, family, or community, inspired, empowered and enabled to creatively plan a strategy for sustained peace and prosperity.'"

The Quaker abolitionist John Woolman also saw a potential problem with success – saying that he wanted to be "free of cumber" and realizing that our work can overwhelm us and consume us, not giving us the time we need to do spiritual work. For Woolman, success included a balanced life.

In one of my more depressed moments about my career and my ability to make a living, my mother told me, "If the only thing you don't have is money, you're way ahead of everyone else!" Influence, joy in one's work, using your talents, loving what you do, finding balance and feeling that the work is bringing us closer to God – all are good indicators of our success and far better indicators than the world's ideas of fame, fortune and power.

35

Obstacles to becoming who we're meant to be

Success seems, in most cases, to be connected to finding our identity, finding out who we are so that we have the confidence to contribute. But our identity can be compromised by both individual and cultural confusion. Thomas Slockee, an Aborigine minister from Australia, says that it took him a while to find success because of a lack of self-confidence which was both individual and cultural: "I grew up with the enemy of an inferiority complex, of low self-worth. As much as I tried to prove myself as good as (what I thought was) the white man's superior ways and culture – in education, sport, nice clothes, etc. – I found that I could never measure up. I always felt looked down on, not as good as. I now know this came from how my parents and the ones before them were treated. How the generations before me were disposed of the land and dispersed from family. There was a loss of identity and traditional culture as well as language and spirituality. All this impacted me, and I was without identity, had a confused spirituality, which stunted me and held me back from realizing my full potential as a human being and as a contributor to the community. It was *only* when Jesus Christ came into my life and I gave up on myself and surrendered to him that my whole life and perspective changed. I was the same as every other human being – I was different but I was equal. I was empowered."

Our inability to find success may not only be an individual problem, but a social problem. Success depends, to a great extent, on the encouragement and nurturing from others, and on the opportunities given to us.

What are we called to do?

Above all, we are called to be in relationship with God. To be sons and daughters of God, doing God's will on earth, building up the Kingdom of God through our work, expressing our spiritual gifts, and being co-creators with God to bring goodness into the world.

Many of us see our careers as a way of expressing attributes of God. For those in the arts, many respond to God the Creator, who makes all things new. We create, we imagine, innovate, bring new worlds into being.

Some identify with Christ the Healer, Sustainer, and Provider who makes those who suffer whole – physically, spiritually, mentally. They work to nourish and heal and maintain the body and soul.

Some express God the Judge, who brings order to the world, working for justice and righteousness and mercy.

Some use their work to express Christ the Liberator, who overcomes oppression and social injustice.

Some feel called to teach, to preach, to interpret, to bring wisdom and understanding. Some feel called to discover the wonders of the creation, or to dig deeply into meaning.

British physicist Wilson Poon sees his work as a way of giving voice to God's creation: "Psalm 19 notes that creation is voiceless (or, more correctly, 'wordless'). I think it is the task of the scientist (amongst others) to 'give voice to creation'. This corresponds well to what Jesus did, particularly in Mark's account. In Jesus' ministry, he repeatedly gave voice to the voiceless. In the case of healing the dumb this is obvious. But in other less obvious cases, we can see it in operation, too. After the woman with the haemorrhage touched his cloak and was healed, he called her out to speak her story. In the case of blind Bartimaeus, the crowds were telling him to shut up when Jesus approached. But Jesus gave him voice (and his sight). So Jesus is the giver of voice to the voiceless. But interestingly, he was practically voiceless in the passion narrative. The one who gave voice became voiceless. So I treat my vocation as a scientist as giving voice to creation but not surprisingly for a Christian, when I am taunted myself, voicelessness is often the only possible response. Painful? You bet! Successful? Not in the world's eyes. Fruitless? Not if I trust that God knows what God is doing."

How are we called?

We find our careers in many ways. Some of you might have experienced a calling to your particular work. Perhaps there has been a nudging, prodding, guiding, or a whisper that pulls you into your life's work. Some speak of "being led" or listening for the gleanings of what we are asked to do.

The idea of a calling is not always neat and clear and each calling demands some discernment. Some might ask: Does God call the equipped or equip the called? Are we always called to what we're good at, or are we sometimes called to do something that will be challenging and stretch our talents?

How do we know when ego is talking, or when we're truly listening to God? How do we sort through social chaos and social expectations to find God's clarity? To what extent does God want us to be prosperous? Do we sometimes get confused because we want our calling to lead us to being respected, perhaps even to wealth, and then realize that is not what our lives are about?

In the deepest part of our soul, we want our lives to express our talents. We want to find meaning through our work. We want to know that what we do counts, and that our lives matter to others. We want to make a difference.

As spiritual people, we also want to feel that we are doing what is the right thing to do – that somehow we are adding to God's work in the world and doing God's will.

Discerning these difficult boundaries is not always easy.

Some callings, of course, do seem clear, and sometimes the passing of time is the best indicator that the calling was clearly from God. Perhaps none is more dramatic than the calling of St. Paul recounted in the Book of Acts. His calling took him through a 180-degree turn from being a persecutor of Christians to being a person considered to be the greatest of all the apostles who spread the word about Christ. Paul is considered to be the first Christian theologian, who helped us understand the meaning of the work of Christ.

By all accounts, Paul was successful as a persecutor of Christians. He seemed to be respected and good at his job. But shortly after the stoning of St. Stephen, Paul was thrown to the ground by a bright light which blinded him and a voice which confronted him about his behavior: "Why do you persecute me?" And then there was a specific order: "Go into town and I will tell you what to do!" He was led into town, made whole again, and was called to preach the gospel.[4]

The Hebrew Scriptures recount the calling of

Samuel, which came not by the dramatic flash that Paul encountered, but a whisper in the night that called to him, "Samuel." This small boy knew little about how to interpret this voice – was it his mother or father calling him? Where was it coming from? His master Eli gave him sound advice: "If he calls you, say 'Speak, Lord, for your servant is listening.'" He was called to a lifetime of service.[5]

Testing and understanding the call

The call comes in many ways and Christians have many ways of defining it. For some, it's a feeling of doing what seems right, what suits them, what they feel compelled to do.

The call uses our talents

Some experience the call as a request. Comedian Torry Martin defines it as "God's personal request for you to work on his agenda using the talents you were given in ways that are significant for His eternal plan." It is a combination of our spiritual gifts used for God's work.

The call makes the formidable possible

Dr. Ted Baehr is the publisher of *Movieguide® Magazine*, which reviews movies from a biblical perspective and which gives awards every year for spiritually uplifting films. Ted is the son of the Hollywood cowboy star Bob "Tex" Allen, who won the Box Office Award in 1936, and of Evelyn Pierce, a star at MGM. He became a lawyer and eventually converted to Christianity when a friend challenged him to read the Bible. Ted says: "Reading even just that part of the Bible changed my perspective, both professionally and personally. A couple of years after my conversion, I went to an Episcopal seminary. Although my father didn't want me to go into the entertainment industry, I was moved by God to help redeem the entertainment industry so that more worthwhile movies and television programs would be produced. God had spoken audibly to me before, but this time it was made plain that it was important to re-establish the church offices that had ushered in the Golden Age of Hollywood. Just doing that alone required the full range of gifts and talents that were given to me in the providential experiences that God had ordained. God's call is always accompanied by significant blessings and victories. When he called, equipped, encouraged, and demanded that I get involved in 'redeeming the values of the mass media', the task looked formidable indeed. There was only one movie when we started *Movieguide®* that had positive, uplifting Christian content. Now, over fifty percent of the films made in Hollywood are filled with such content. God promises that when we accept Jesus we will have life more abundantly, including trials and tribulations. And he has governed every step along the way."

The call is accepted and recognized through prayer

Actor Denzel Washington recognizes that he has been called to do his work: "I understand that what I've been blessed to do is a part of God's plan." He begins every film with a prayer he learned from his mother: "Heavenly Father, We come before thee, knee bent and body bowed, in the humblest way that we know how." Washington

41

says, "I open the film with a prayer and end it with praise." When asked about his film, *The Great Debaters*, he said, "Every major decision I made, I made through prayer, about who I was picking to be in it, what it was I was trying to say, praying that the film was saying the right thing and that it would reach the right people ... It's how I start every day, and it's how I end every day."[6] Washington describes himself as having "an ongoing conversation with God."[7]

The call asks us to be good stewards

Singapore businessman Ken Swee felt called to be an investment advisor. He says: "I know God has a plan for me in the market place. It is a calling as a sparkler and to help others and to encourage them in Biblical finance as well. In my job I meet a lot of people and I help my clients in investments. Often I know I am dealing with many of my clients' life savings. It is a big responsibility. I take it personally like a steward and a shepherd to help protect and grow it. I do like to help Christian investors especially and one of the things is to help them learn to give to Kingdom expansion not just in money but in other areas of time, influence, evangelism, love and missions outside of church. I believe this is a multiplication effect from what one could do by themselves."

The call may be twofold

Scientist D. Gareth Jones believes that he had two related callings – "the first into science and the second into academic life. While these two overlap they are not the same.

"My calling into science was a calling into scientific research. In my second year as a medical student, my intention was to become a clinician of some description. I had never thought about anything else. In fact, I didn't know about anything else. However, it was then that I discovered the world of scientific research. I went into a seminar on the structure of the cell membrane, knowing next to nothing about scientific research, and I emerged knowing that this is what I wanted to do in life. The seminar had the goal of introducing medical students to the world of research and I for one was instantly hooked. For me it was not unlike a conversion experience; my eyes had been opened, and a world I had never previously encountered was to become an integral part of all I was to do from that point onwards.

"More specifically my calling was into study of the nervous system, the brain in particular. This was determined by the department in which I learned my trade, but it also fitted neatly into my Christian perspective. On the one hand, the brain is the most complex, fascinating and perplexing aspect of our bodies and of what we are as persons. Consequently, it presents an immense intellectual challenge to all who study it or even think much about it. For me the dimensions of this challenge have been stimulating rather than overwhelming, since I have been constantly reminded of the creative dimensions of what we all are as people made in the image of God. Attempting to unravel just a few of the mysteries of the brain and how it functions has been deeply meaningful as one comes face-to-face with the abiding mystery of our existence as thinking, worshipping beings.

"Alongside this reason for studying the brain is the allied one of wanting to work towards helping those, both now and in the future, who suffer from the ravages of the various neurodegenerative diseases. The destructiveness of the neurodegenerative diseases robs people of the glory and grandeur of human personhood. The dementias in particular are horrifying in the manner in which they remove from individuals the higher capabilities that characterize the human condition. When people are no longer able to respond to each other, let alone to God, they become far less than they should be. If only we could prevent this happening or even slow it, we would be participating in one of the most precious tasks there is in health care. While researchers like me may not be dealing directly with patients, the hope is that our work will contribute in some small way towards the eventual resolution of some of these horrifying conditions. In other words, our goal is to make a contribution, no matter how small, towards an endeavor with immense repercussions for good. Of course, practically none of us makes dramatic discoveries, but we are helping to advance understanding, and this constitutes the core of what I have seen as my calling in neuroscience.

"The second calling I have had is into academic life. For some this is regarded as an erudite and highly questionable enterprise. Not for me. Basic to research is critical analysis, something that lies at the root of every aspect of my life, my science, and my Christian faith. The willingness and ability to ask questions is, for me, little less than a sacred task, since it has the potential of getting us closer to the truth.

"The academic life has meant having one's assumptions and preconceptions as a Christian challenged, and this I have found enlivening and positive, as long as my own spiritual base is firm and well established.

"And then there are students, bright minds, young minds, some lost, some on a definite upward trajectory. And the best are challenging, asking awkward questions, na ve questions, penetrating questions. To see young people changed and mature is a blessing, as education in the best sense transforms and builds character. Of course, it is not always like this; there are disappointments as potential is dashed or wasted. But the successes are to be cherished, as I am able to discern my place in a sacred, character building exercise."

The call has far-reaching implications

British scientist Andrew Gosler defines his call as "to reduce the rate of biodiversity loss, and to teach people the value of all life, non-human as well as human." He sees this work as relating to both scientific, and larger social issues. "It was when I realized that in fact biodiversity loss globally was inextricably linked with issues of human injustice, unfair trade practices and human poverty, together with a re-evaluation of the meaning of Genesis (the big picture) that I realized that our salvation globally was linked to the need for humility, and that Christ was indeed the key. This required a spiritual growth that I had never known, but all these things together have given me a sense of the wholeness of Creation."

The call brings purpose and usually joy

For others, the calling is not specific, but is proven by the joy and personal growth and impact that results. Lisa Borden is a missionary in Tanzania for an organization called Wild Hope International. Wild Hope partners with local efforts to bring transformation and hope to Africa. Lisa saw her calling, first, in general terms: "I cannot say

45

that I felt a distinct call at a clear point in my life that directed me to Africa or even to what some would refer to as missionary work. What I *did* feel was a sense (a calling?) that my life would be about serving others. The only question I had, really, is what form that service would take. Nursing seemed like a practical choice that could take me anywhere as health care is needed everywhere. However, my high school science grades convinced me that this was probably not going to be my field.

"I like to say that I went to Africa because I was in love with a boy who wanted to be there. While that might have been my initial reason to move to Kenya with my young husband, I remained because I thrived there. I found purpose, passion and joy in the work we took up. My father had always advised us that when it comes to making decisions about things of this nature, we should do what we are willing and able to do that others are not willing and able to do. Thriving in a location and vocation with joy and personal growth while feeling satisfied that my work makes a difference is all the confirmation of a calling that I need."

Figuring out the calling

I have had three different experiences that felt like a clear calling to my work. When I was nineteen, I loved drama, but was not very good at it. Others were better actors, received better grades in classes, were simply more dramatic personalities. Yet, I was happiest when acting, reading plays, even directing theater. One day, as I stood in my dorm room, I asked God how I could enter this field, since I wasn't a natural in drama. I heard a quiet voice inside my head say, "Your job is to keep the dream of drama alive!" I knew immediately what that voice meant, since I had felt, on some not-quite-articulated level, that drama was one of the greatest of the humanities and that it could inspire us, reveal the human condition, and had the potential to encourage us and to lift up our dreams and hopes. I realized that was what I was to do – in one form or another.

A few years later, after getting an MA in Drama and teaching college, I felt there was still much to explore, but didn't know where to go for further graduate work. There were few universities that offered a PhD in drama in the early 1970s and none of them interested me. I heard that a seminary in Berkeley had studies in drama and theology, but wasn't sure about getting such an unmarketable degree. In my confusion about how to find some answers, I went forward at an altar call at the small Baptist college where I was teaching (Grand Canyon College in Phoenix, Arizona). I had no idea, at that moment, about the significance of this rather humiliating act, but one of my Christian friends encouraged me not to discount the experience. Two days later, as I turned my car onto the freeway on my way to work, I suddenly knew that I was going to seminary.

I went to visit Pacific School of Religion in Berkeley, California to reinforce the decision, and was still pondering over this decision when I read in the book of Acts the words, "go into the city and I will tell you what to do!" The words were given to Paul, but I felt they were also meant for me, so I decided to see where they would lead me. I went to the university campus several blocks away from the seminary, figuring that was the center of the city, sat down in the library, and waited while flipping through a magazine to see who would tell me what to do. Several moments later, a man came up to me and asked if I wanted to go outside and talk. Deciding that this was supposed to be an angelic voice, and not a pick-up line, we went outside, I told him about my indecision and he said, "Come to Berkeley! You're ready!" So I went. And that decision changed the direction of my life.

Many others have found that their leading came through specific Bible verses or through other inspiring words.

Andi S. Boediman is an entrepreneur in creative education in Jakarta, Indonesia, where he runs a creative communication school. He was continually called and led through various Bible verses which spoke to him. He says, "I had worked very hard on my undergraduate study in architecture, but the result was just OK, not what I expected. I was emotionally and physically very tired. One day my sister invited me to a local church and I got my Born Again experience. When pursuing my graduate education in design, I decided to write a book on digital imaging and was encouraged by Ecclesiastes 11:6, which says, 'Sow your seed in the morning and do not be idle in the evening, for you do not know whether morning or evening sowing will succeed, or whether both of them alike will be good.' Out of this book, I started to be invited to speak and share my knowledge in computer graphics and started to give seminars, training programs, and lectures. My design practice was also running pretty good because people trusted me after seeing my book. Then, in 1998, there were big riots in Indonesia, and as a Chinese, a lot of us felt very discouraged to stay in Indonesia. In 1999, I went to New York for further study in Film Production. A few friends prayed for me and they gave me the revelation that I should get into education. I was very reluctant to go back to Indonesia, but then I found this verse from Jonah 4:11: 'Should I not have compassion on Nineveh, the great city in which there are more than 120,000 persons who do not know the difference between their right and left hand, as well as many animals?' I decided I should not judge my country and I should be the one to make a difference. I started Digital Studio Creative Education. Now, more than 15,000 people have attended our workshops and seminars."

For Jim and Karen Covell, their leading came from St. Augustine. Both Jim and Karen work in the Hollywood film industry – Jim as a composer (he composed the music for the films *Left Behind*, *The Ride*, and *McGee and Me*) and Karen as a producer. Both found inspiration from St. Augustine's words, "Love God and do what you will!" Karen explains: "I never felt 'called' to do my work as a producer. I just wanted to do that. I believe that if we seek God then we will want to do what he wants us to do. I believe God gave me gifts and talents and when I use them, he gets the glory and I feel his pleasure! After I committed to forming the Hollywood Prayer Network, because I really wanted to, I saw that it was the right thing to do and I was confirmed many times over that this is what I believe is God's plan for my life."

Some don't think of this prodding as a call, but more as a leading or finally finding something that seems to suit them, and that can help them find meaning and do good in the world.

For all, this nudge led them to finding a way to express their gifts and express the work of the Spirit.

Recognizing one's gifts

We are called to use our gifts. This begins with the confidence that we have gifts, and with some recognition of what those gifts might be. Like Karen and Jim Covell, Douglas Millham looks at what attracts him, and what type of discernment he has. "I am a person drawn to crisis – to people, churches, groups, nations, tribes, families – which are fragile, hurting, vulnerable or wounded, where the presence of love, compassion, encouragement can assist in bringing these people to a transcendent and transforming moment of experiencing God's love, peace and presence."

Douglas sees his gifts have developed over the years, doing the work he feels called to do. "Over the years, I've become an expert in reading people – of all backgrounds, ages, cultures – reading their motives, actions, goals, discerning their ethics, values, integrity. Separating the followers of God from the fakers, the real from the pretenders, the maneuvers from the manipulators, the simply misled from the truly evil and corrupt. This is a heavy burden and a tremendous gift in my profession, which is connecting the resources of a compassionate world with the needs of vulnerable and hurting children and communities."

But what about...???

How do we absolutely know we are following the calling of God? We probably can't. Our lives are grounded in a flawed world. The cacophony of the world might distort it. Our desires may push us into thinking we're doing the right thing, but we may be on a detour or a side road or going in the wrong direction without knowing it. Jim Covell explains how we sometimes misinterpret the call: "Some who have heard 'the call' may have gotten the wrong number or at least a bad cell-phone connection."

How can we be sure we've received the call clearly? In his book *Essays on the Quaker Vision of Gospel Order*, Lloyd Lee Wilson discusses several different tests we can do to test the call and help ourselves discern if we're on the right path.

Test the call by waiting first

He recommends we first simply wait and not feel rushed: "The first thing to do ... is nothing at all. One simply sits with the incipient leading, tasting it in the silence of one's personal worship and devotional time, waiting to see whether it feels true and if so, how it will develop. This is a time to be, rather than to do: to be listening to the Divine voice, to be quiet in one's worldly activities, to be ready to hear and obey."[8] God is not in a rush. God is not frenetic. Meanwhile, the adversary to our call wants to get us in a tizzy, running in all sorts of different directions, and wants us to be confused and hopes we misinterpret the call. Waiting centers us. It gets us in tune with the Spirit and with the still waters rather than the rushing rapids.

The call will reinforce the gospel

A call will not contradict the essential gospel message: "True leadings guide us in ways that are in harmony with the Spirit that gave forth the Scriptures and with the clear teachings of Christ," says Wilson.[9] And he says a call will not contradict the paths we've taken before that have seemed in tune with the Spirit. "A true leading should feel like a continuation of other movements in our spiritual life that have proven to have been Spirit-led and Spirit-fed."[10]

The call will express spiritual gifts

A call will manifest and express the gifts of the Spirit – such as love, joy, peace, patience, kindness, goodness, trustfulness, gentleness and self-control.[11] St. Paul adds a long list of characteristics which are contrary to the Spirit. We would not be called to be nasty, hateful, back-biting, gossiping, mean-spirited, self-indulgent, jealous, quarrelsome, malicious, or antagonistic.[12] If we don't find joy and peace in the work we do, and aren't adding love and kindness through our work, we might need to question whether this is a true calling.

A call would use our spiritual gifts. St. Paul lists a number of gifts we might have, such as the gift of wisdom, of healing, of prophecy, of discernment,[13] of teaching, and of service.[14] From our own experience, we could add others – the gifts of the artist, the scientist, the businessperson, those who do social service, those who administer, among others. Wilson suggests our spiritual gifts are not only discerned by us, but we can turn to our spiritual community to help us discern our gifts. He warns: "spiritual gifts are subtle, especially when they first appear, and our ability to recognize and name them is easily confused by our personal hopes, fears, wishes ... We also have an Adversary who is actively working against the Gospel Order, and whose best defense against the effectiveness of the spiritual gifts God has given the people of faith is to prevent us from recognizing them at all or naming them properly."[15] Our spiritual community can help us name our gifts, but also encourage us to be good stewards of our gifts, even when we are tempted to doubt them, or dismiss them, or to compromise them. Our spiritual community can help support us in our recognition and use of them, can help us find opportunities for using them, and can help us develop the gifts and be proper stewards of the talents we've been given.

The call brings us harmony and peace

A call brings us into harmony with God, and brings us a sense of peace, release, relief, and clarity. Quakers sometimes use the words "to be at ease" with a decision. Others might describe it as being comfortable, or as a kind of knowing that feels solid. Wilson says, "True ministry does bring personal change as we are shaped to the task we have been given and have accepted, and brought into closer harmony with the One who shapes us."[16] Wilson encourages us not to be afraid of change, but to recognize that God is with us through difficult situations and won't forsake us. The change God asks of us brings us closer "to becoming that person whom God created us to become."

Wilson suggests we ask the question: "can [we] envision Christ deeply involved in this ministry if he were present among us bodily once again?"[17]

Our call can be discerned by others

To test the call, some might turn for advice to spiritual people they trust, who they believe have a gift of discernment. This may be a pastor or wise friend, or it may be a group of people who gather to help them find clarity about a direction they're considering. Some Quakers form a Clearness Committee where they can ask questions about a perceived call in order to find clarity and discern the right direction. Together, they test the spirits and look for the clarity and unity the Spirit brings. And when it feels right? Rather than be like Jonah who ran away from it, we would hope we would follow it. Wilson says, "we should offer no more resistance than a dandelion seed, lifted by the breeze to a new place in creation."[18]

Is the calling effective and successful?

Many callings seem to prove they are right by the effectiveness of the work. Few would probably doubt Billy Graham's calling to be an evangelist. Or Albert Schweitzer's calling to help the sick in Africa. Or Mother Theresa's calling to care for the dying in Calcutta.

But effectiveness is not always the test of whether it's a true calling. Isaiah was called to be a prophet, knowing his work would not really yield fruit in his lifetime. Some musicians, and artists, didn't really make their mark until after their deaths. Some may do work that is done on a small scale – there are no riches, or huge crowds of people to praise the work or to prove its importance. The success of our work cannot be determined simply by numbers.

In the film business, it's often said one doesn't know whether there's a possibility of being successful – at selling a script, making a movie, getting a good job – until someone has tried for at least five years. This is often true for other careers as well. Few people find real success overnight. For many, it takes five years or more just to get started in a career – to do the preparation, to learn what has to be learned. Few develop mastery without working at it for ten or twenty years. The test of time is not always the best test.

Our success is not determined by numbers, or praise, or awards, or riches, or by how quickly everything goes our way.

And sometimes we don't know for sure. All we can do is to be obedient to what we discern our calling to be. And to move, step by step, along the path and to keep listening to the Spirit which may often be only a still small voice within a confused and chaotic world. We follow the light we have, hoping for a clear "yes" to continue, or a clear "no" to stop and turn in another direction. We try to commit to manifesting the Spirit in the world, knowing our steps and our work may still be flawed.

The twin layers of success

Although we often think of our success in terms of our ability to perform our work well, and achieve, accomplish, and do well, there is another layer of success that comes from what we put into our work apart from our specific skills and abilities.

We are called not just to specific jobs, but we are called to express the Holy Spirit through our work. So often I've met people who think of their jobs as, perhaps, lowly, or simple, or not very important. Yet, my days are blessed by the warmth and kindness of the woman who takes in my dry cleaning, the person at the grocery store who makes sure I find what I need, the receptionist at the doctor's office who cares about my well-being. Every job has those people in it who bring something more than simply their skills – they also bring a sense of caring, compassion, sensitivity, kindness. They express the Spirit not just through the work, but through something else they bring which is an intrinsic part of their identity and spirituality.

Joni Harms is a Country-Western singer who threads her spirituality into her music. One of my favorite songs is her song, "Millie", about a waitress whose work and personality clearly blessed Joni's own work. Joni recounts her first time meeting Millie. "I will never forget the first time I met Millie (not her real name) at the Pancake Pantry in Nashville, Tennessee. I was having breakfast there with all the big dogs from Capitol Records (I had just been signed as a new recording artist there) and we were all going out together to talk about a marketing plan for "the cowgirl from Canby, Oregon". I was very nervous as you can imagine wanting to say and do everything correctly.

All of a sudden here came Millie to our table and right away she said, "Well who do we have here today?" She obviously knew all of the Capitol Records crew as the Pancake Pantry was one of their favorite hangouts in Nashville. I was introduced to Millie, who took my order while smiling sweetly at me the whole time. All of a sudden my fear went away and a wonderful calmness came over me. I watched her while I ate my breakfast and saw the effect she had on other people as well.

A month or two later I was back in Nashville writing songs for my up and coming album. I called the writer I was working with that day and ask if they minded meeting for breakfast at the Pancake Pantry just hoping Millie might be there to wait on our table. They were happy to start the day with a good breakfast so we both arrived there around 9:30.

The place was very busy as usual. I ask if by chance Millie was working that morning and if so, might we be seated in her section. Sure enough, there she was. She seemed to see me too and smiled as if she remembered me.

Within a few minutes we were seated in her section. She came quickly to our table and said, "Well hello Joni Harms, how are things in Oregon? Glad you're back!" She even remembered what I ordered and asked if I would like to have it again. Needless to say this made quite an impression on me and I ended up writing a song about her with the co-writer of some of my songs, Wood Newton. Millie really took pride in her work. She seemed to realize that even a waitress could make a difference in people's lives! We wrote a line for the song that said why Millie was so special – "she brought more to the table than the order she was taking."[19] It isn't just the work we do, but how well we express the spiritual dimension of life.

The Spirit and the world

What do we know about the spiritual world? It's a world without limits. We can dream in this world. We aren't held down by the weight of the physical which defines us as ordinary, as mere humans, as someone determined by our class, gender, culture, or economics.

Those who live by the Spirit have a different set of goals and values for their careers. Like everyone, we are tempted by the things of the world. But the Spirit guides us into seeing our lives differently, so our work is not just a set of things to do to bring us adulation and wealth, but a motivation from deep inside us that brings us happiness and contentment.

The world loves us when we're clever and smart. The Spirit asks us to be wise.

The world brings us money. The Spirit brings us blessings of abundance and prosperity.

The world admires us for our success. The Spirit loves us and nourishes our work.

The world keeps pulling us into its value system – of money, fortune, ego gratification, and being just a little bit better than everyone else.

The Spirit keeps whispering to us about meaning – about contributing and doing something to help others. About using our God-given talents to make a difference. About choosing for the long term, not the short term.

The President of Pacific School of Religion, Dr. Davie Napier, said at my graduation ceremony when I received my ThD, "You know you're on the way to the Promised Land by the fear you feel when you take the first step." Even when we know what we want, and feel determined to get it, there is still fear and temptation and side alleys and dead ends as we step out on the road.

But, for many, there is a point where things get easier. When it seems that maybe the dream we were after has finally become possible.

And when we've arrived at our goals?

We wait for that moment when we feel we've arrived. We've made it. We've reached our peak and hit our stride. We've realized our dreams and goals and now we can coast. After years of struggle, we feel we're at the top of our game, the best we can be. But it's not over yet – not at all. The spiritual issues merely change.

When we're taking the steps to success, we are dependent on the Spirit to help us overcome the anxieties, the uncertainties, the doubts. We try to have faith in the future and belief in ourselves. We keep the dream before us and our belief that somehow it's possible, with God's help. We are vulnerable and need God's comfort. We are doubtful, and need to be bolstered by faith. We are needy, and need God's help. We get up every morning and somehow go on, hoping but not knowing the outcome.

Then, at some point, when we achieve success, sometimes beyond our wildest and craziest dreams, our whole relationship with God changes. We don't think we need God. We are doing just fine on our own. We don't need his comfort. We now have all the comfort money can buy. We have no more doubts. We have proven the dream is worthwhile. Our pride bolsters us up. The respect of others convinces us all is well and we are no longer vulnerable. Everything that seemed to be part of our relationship with God is no longer relevant.

But doubts do come. Sometimes, we might feel that just as everything is going well, the rug will be pulled out from under our happy feet. This leaves us unsure about our success and we begin to wonder whether we've achieved our success at the expense of our spiritual lives. If we no longer seem to need God, then what kind of relationship can we have?

I struggled with this question when I started my business. As success began to seem a possibility, I realized it may not be in God's best interests to prosper me if I lost my spiritual direction. I had no idea what other kind of spiritual relationship was possible, since my relationship with God was dependent, rather than interdependent. I realized I may have painted myself into a corner by having a big dream, and then lost what was most important in life to achieve it. What do we gain in the world if we lose what makes it fulfilling?

I decided to pray about this, and told God, "Although I don't know what kind of relationship we'll have in the future, and I know it will be different, I promise not to desert you when I become successful. I'll continue to read the Bible, pray, and go to my Quaker Meeting, even though I don't understand where we're going. I will pledge obedience, even when I have no understanding of exactly what new relationship this will become."

As my business began to prosper, I kept this promise. Even so, it took me three years to re-form my relationship with God.

When I achieved my goals and my dreams, I began to understand some central concepts about spiritual and material success and how they fit together.

It can be, and might be, in God's best interest to prosper us, if we are doing God's work and nurturing our spiritual life. There is no reason for the rug to be pulled out from under us if we're doing good in the world. Of course, it can happen. Life doesn't always go according to plan, and tragedy can strike even when things are going well. But the Spirit does not want our failure. He wants our success, provided it doesn't damage our relationship with what is most important in life, and provided our success can serve the Kingdom, and provided the sign of

God's favor is not based on how much wealth we have. Prosperity may, or may not, include material blessings. It is meant to include the abundant life, and the sweetness of God's peace and love, no matter the circumstances.

The ups and downs that come on the road to success, and on the arrival at the goal, are not necessarily part of God's plan, but might be part of the natural course of events. God may not want us to struggle, but the business of success usually includes overcoming barriers on the way – whether or not they are part of God's making. It is realistic to have doubts, to have some downturns in business now and then, to have some months that are good and some that are not. Just because we hit some snags along the way doesn't mean we're not on the right path.

At the same time, we need to recognize that doors do close in our careers. New directions may open up. We may need to make changes. Perhaps the greatest challenge is to discern when we're to move on and when we're to work harder.

There is no such thing as arrival. It's never over. We need continued blessings, and are continually dependent on God, day by day, in order to do what we've been called to do.

Although the road to success may be rocky and hard, the arrival is usually sweet. But for the spiritual person, the walk is never over.

Expanding our identities

Change is the only constant in life. We either grow or slow. There is no such thing as arriving, standing still, simply maintaining. Although the world may want us to remain the same, the Spirit asks us to keep growing.

There is a prayer in the Hebrew Scriptures called the Prayer of Jabez. Jabez asked God to bless him, and that God would "expand my territories", sometimes translated as "enlarge my coast."[20] Since success could be defined as being effective at doing good in the world, we are continually expanding our identities and our possibilities through a ripple effect outward. Our inner lives and our outer lives can always make more of a difference with others. The more clout and power we have, the more potential there is for what we do to change the world for the better.

With success comes responsibility. Jesus said, "When someone is given a great deal, a great deal will be demanded of that person; when someone is entrusted with a great deal, of that person even more will be expected."[21] The more we get, the more we're expected to give.

We are never finished people. We are never completed. We are never perfected. We are always in the process of becoming bigger people.

We might want to maintain and sit back, and there's nothing wrong with relaxing and having less anxiety, but we are still in movement. We are still becoming. We are still building on our success for a greater good.

We become greater contributors to life. Our decisions as we expand are not based on our self-interest, but on the bigger picture. We don't just think of ourselves, but judge business decisions by whether they seem good for something greater than ourselves. We try to add value and expand value. We are constantly in the process of expanding our identities.

To combine our business lives and our spiritual lives still takes another element to make it work – it takes the leap of faith.

Questions for reflection and discussion

1. Have you experienced a call or leading to your work? What was it? Did it seem clear to you, or did you question it?
2. What has proven to you that this call came from God?
3. Have there been important Bible verses or theological ideas or inspirational words that reinforced this call?
4. Who has supported, perhaps even helped, you define your call? Your friends? Spouse? Spiritual community? Family? Have there been adversaries to your call? How have you defined them? As evil? Uninformed? Unimaginative? How have you overcome them?
5. Has it been difficult to maintain your call? Or has the call made it possible for you to continue even when there were difficulties?

Scripture to consider

Read the stories about the calling of the disciples (Matthew 4; Luke 5), Paul (Acts 7; 9) and Samuel (1 Samuel 3).

✱ Kan ik die verantwoordelijkheid aan? Kan ik het dragen?
Hoe help ik Pollo aan zijn film?

CHAPTER 2

The Leap of Faith

Why does taking the leap of faith look so easy?

Søren Kierkegaard[22]

There is nothing very complicated about it ... you merely step out on the springboard and the leap comes automatically!

Friedrich Heinrich Jacobi[23]

A preliminary running start helps to make the leap easier.

Søren Kierkegaard[24]

One of the great Protestant theologians of the nineteenth century, Søren Kierkegaard, says it takes a leap of faith to move into the world of Spirit. In fact, it takes a leap of faith to move into any endeavor. The future is never assured. The ending is never known.

Those of us who confess to a spiritual life believe in the existence of an Unseen Force which we might call God or Yahweh or Father or the Almighty or any one of many ways to address God. If you read the verses about faith in the Bible, you will find most of them ask us to have faith in God, or faith in Jesus Christ as the Son of God. We take these verses at face value and translate our faith into belief statements: "I believe in God the Father Almighty, maker of heaven and earth, and in Jesus Christ, his only begotten Son …"[25] But we believe in more than that – we believe in certain attributes of the Unseen. We name the little voice and the inner call which almost everyone experiences at some time. And we believe God can be spoken to and God speaks to us.

There are many ways to understand the attributes of God, and the way we understand God determines how we see the object of our faith. Some believe in a God who is vengeful and harsh, even sometimes petty and cruel, and they have faith God will not act kindly to them if they cross certain boundaries of behavior.

Others believe this Presence is loving and powerful and personal. They have faith that God can intervene in history, and can act on their behalf, and is forgiving and loving, in spite of their many flaws.

Faith begins with faith in something unseen. Faith is not about proof, it is its antithesis. Faith sees the world and our lives from another viewpoint. We might define faith as paying attention to the Unseen Loving Power which we believe in and try to allow to lead our lives. As time goes on, and we grow in faith, we develop a greater sense of the Unseen Presence. We listen to it and for it, and we begin to trust that this Dependable Power will come through for us. We may feel its presence through the spiritual energy we feel in church, in the middle of a rousing hymn, or with others of our faith who share their compassion, and we feel their love. Some call this experience one of feeling light, or feeling comforted, or feeling loved, or feeling safe, or feeling cared for. We might experience this Power as a guide. We sense we are being led in a certain direction, or told, in some way, where we are to go.

That experience then moves us back to a clearer

sense of who God is. We use specific names for God to describe the Presence we can trust – the Light Within, the Comforter, the Beloved, the Savior, the Compassionate One, the Lord and Shepherd, the Guide. We learn to call on God, and learn to have faith that the response will be one of love, comfort, safety, and guidance.

God may seem, many times, to be amorphous, but over the course of some time, we begin to sense a Presence, a Profound Depth worth listening to, that guides our actions and leads us to express our best selves, and to express the Spirit within us.

Making the leap

What is this leap of faith? It begins without knowing much about this God we are turning to. Yet, in spite of not being able to see or touch or feel God, we try to live our lives differently, and to live with a sense of God's presence and guidance and comfort. This often means trusting when we have no idea what or who we're trusting in. We don't know what the result of our trust will be, nor how much, nor how little, to trust in God, nor how much, nor how little, to trust in ourselves. Yet, it is exactly this movement into the unknown that can set our path and eventually lead us to clearly knowing what God wants of us.

Some have radical trust and place themselves fully in the hands of God. It is said some of the early Irish monks and saints, including St. Brendan, would sail forth on the great seas in a little, round, skin-covered boat without sails, and trust to God to deliver them to the land of his choosing. And, it seemed, he did.

Physicist Wilson Poon sees the leap of faith as an intrinsic part of any work, but especially the work of science. He says: "To turn evidence into an interesting hypothesis *always* requires a leap of faith. A good scientist is one who can make these leaps successfully. Many apprentice scientists *never* succeed in making such leaps, they are too scared. A 'good' leap is a well-founded leap. I can give reasons for my faith but it is a leap nevertheless. And leaps are costly – I have to commit time and resources to seek out the consequences of the leap. I have to live, sometimes for years, as if the leap is true, but with little tangible evidence to tell me I am right. Sometimes all the evidence seems to point the other way. But I persist, partly because I had strong reasons to make the leap in the first place. In the end, I am sometimes wrong. But quite often, I prove right, but not from the directions I had expected initially."

The leap may move us to different conclusions and surprises. It might take our careers into different directions. It might push us into new commitments.

Many of our great religious leaders have had to make this leap of faith with regard to their life's work, sometimes amidst great inner turmoil when trying to find God's will for their lives.

Billy Graham wanted to be a baseball player. There were two things he clearly did not want to be – a preacher or an undertaker. As a student at Florida Bible Institute, he was asked by one of his teachers to preach, and had little recourse but to go along with the command. He was nervous, and simply not very good. In fact, many predicted failure for Billy as a preacher, although he seemed to do well as a Fuller Brush salesman. Gradually, he began to feel he was being called to be an evangelist.

When he began working with the greatest evangelist of the day, Charles Templeton, and began a friendship with him as well, his faith was tested when Templeton gave up his ministry, announced himself as an agnostic, and told Billy that he was committing "intellectual suicide" and was "50 years out of date" by believing the Bible.[26] Charles told Billy his faith was too simple: "People no longer accept the Bible as being inspired the way you do."[27]

Templeton threw the baby out with the bathwater, believing it was not possible to reconcile the Bible and his Christian faith, and felt he had to give up both. In giving up both, he also gave up the work he once felt called to do. Yet Billy had built his career on his faith in the Bible. Billy says, "I wanted to keep abreast of theological [ideas] but brilliant writers such as Karl Barth and Reinhold Niebuhr really made me struggle with concepts that had been ingrained in me since childhood ... the particular intellectual problem I was wrestling with for the first time since my conversion as a teenager was the inspiration and authority of the Scriptures ... I was the President of a liberal arts college, Bible school and seminary – an institution whose doctrinal statement was extremely strong and clear on this point ... Feeling a little hypocritical, I began an intensive study of this question. I read theologians and scholars on all sides of this issue. I also turned to the Bible itself[28] ... I got up and took a walk. ... I opened the Bible at random on a tree stump in front of me ... The exact wording of my prayer is beyond recall, but it must have echoed my thoughts: 'Oh God! There are many things in this book I do not understand. There are many problems with it for which I have no solution. There are many seeming contradictions

...' At last the Holy Spirit freed me to say it. 'Father, I am going to accept this as Thy Word – by faith.' ... In my heart and mind, I knew a spiritual battle in my soul had been fought and won."[29]

That was 1949. Billy went on to preach the Bible and the salvation message of God in over 100 countries to millions of people. Billy confronted God, and chose to take the leap of faith and believe in God's Word. His work prospered, and he has been known as the leading evangelist of his time for over fifty years.[30]

Billy Graham and Charles Templeton represent two different, almost opposite ways of dealing with the difficulties of faith. Mother Theresa also experienced the turmoils of faith as she tried to find her vocation.

She had a vision of Jesus in 1946. She is quoted in the book, *Come Be My Light*, as saying Jesus called her to abandon teaching and work in the slums of the city, dealing with the poorest of the poor. She felt Jesus called her to "Come, come, carry Me into the holes of the poor. Come be My Light." After she had the vision, she wrote, cajoled, and pleaded with the Catholic Church to allow her to follow this vision, and when they finally said "yes", it seemed Jesus disappeared. For the rest of her life, aside from a few times, she experienced the deepest Dark Night of the Soul, and a sense of emptiness and longing for Christ. Although she never re-found the vision, she continued to do what she felt called to do. She never gave up on giving love, even when it seemed she had little to cling to.[31]

Although she felt uncertain about her faith, even sometimes distrusting the existence of God and heaven in the years that followed, she stayed true to this calling and became one of the most respected and beloved people of the twentieth century. The one vision sustained her, along with her belief and faith in the power of love and her responsibility toward her vocation. In one of her prayers, she says: "Sweetest Lord, make me appreciative of the dignity of my high vocation, and its many responsibilities. Never permit me to disgrace it by giving way to coldness, unkindness, or impatience."[32]

Many of the people who inspire us have felt led in their work, and yet had struggles and challenges with their faith.

Nelson Mandela continued to have faith that his sacrifices could help overcome the evils of apartheid. His twenty-seven years in prison became a symbol of the unyielding faith in the possibility of goodness and reconciliation.

Archbishop Romero had faith that justice for the poor was possible in El Salvador, and gave his life for his faith.

Martin Luther King, Jr. had faith that black and white could live together in peace. "Take the first step in faith," he said. "You don't have to see the whole staircase, just take the first step."[33]

The Bible is filled with stories of the struggles and victories of faith: "It was by faith that Noah … took care to build an ark", and through faith Abraham "obeyed the call to set out for a country that was the inheritance given to him and his descendants … by faith he sojourned in the Promised Land … It was by faith Moses … left Egypt without fear of the king's anger, he held to his purpose like someone who could see the Invisible … It was through faith the walls of Jericho fell down."[34]

Like many of these people of faith, there are times

we are confronted with a mystery, or a question, or a conflict we don't understand, and yet, that demands a response from us. At times we reach resolution and peace through this leap of faith. Other times, our faith leads us to further questioning, further struggle, and to new conclusions and new decisions.

Eventually many of us have some experience of God which is no longer simply a leap, but a type of silent and sweet knowing. But faith is faith, because it is not tangible and rarely feels absolute. It includes doubt as well. Sometimes our faith seems well founded and our hopes to do good work come to fruition. We listen to God's leading, follow it, and our lives seem to be blessed. It seems God is leading us to a new location. We go. And we're more successful and happier. We feel called to a new job. We follow the call and we seem to be more effective. We begin to have faith in God's leading because when we follow it, it seems to yield a more blessed life.

But sometimes it doesn't work that way. We have faith that our kind and spiritual colleagues will come through for us in times of trouble. And sometimes they don't. We have faith that if we feel guided to move to another city, and move there, this move will be happy and successful. And sometimes it isn't. We have faith we chose the right employee for our project and we discover our employee has a mean streak which we never noticed before. We have faith the business partner who seemed to be God-sent will help prosper our business, but the partner embezzles our money.

Were we wrong? Were we hard of hearing? Or, might we have misinterpreted our faith?

The sometimes misguiding power of faith

In my work in the film industry, I've worked with hundreds of Christian writers. Most of them feel guided by God to write. And they have faith in the outcome. The writer writes a novel, and has faith it will sell and even become successful. The screenwriter writes a script, and has faith it will eventually become a major motion picture. The non-fiction writer writes a book and communicates ideas, and has faith it will be published and find a readership that will change lives.

Along this faith journey, some writers look for easy answers, believing if they just write the first draft, all will be well because God will make everything wonderful. Other writers recognize the faith journey takes preparation, sometimes a steep learning curve, learning how to market their work, meeting the right people. They pray for guidance along the way, and sometimes it seems as if their faith is being fulfilled. They're led to the right teachers, to the right books, and sometimes feel led to an interested producer or publisher who wants to buy their work. Sometimes, all goes well.

But sometimes, in spite of following the Guide, things don't turn out. The script doesn't get sold. The book may get published, but no one reads it, and it soon goes out of print. No matter how hard we try, or how hard we pray, sometimes success eludes us. We might ask, "Was I wrong when I began to follow this path, or is it that God simply doesn't care? Or did I simply misinterpret my Guide?"

This may be where we make our mistakes in the relationship of our faith to our profession. We have faith in our work, instead of in our mysterious God. We believe God wants what we want, and if we just learn what we need to know to be successful in our field, and then work hard, everything will turn out just fine. We have faith in a process others in our field have told us will lead to success. We have faith in our intelligence, our creativity, our abilities, and our colleagues. We add some spirituality to that process – some prayer, some church-going, perhaps a fast or a sacrifice to give us some extra added leverage for success. And when it doesn't work out, we question our faith, we question our God, we question ourselves, and we end up stymied and puzzled and disillusioned.

This is one of the great mysteries of faith. We expect faith to eventually bail us out and to make everything right. We believe in the process that leads us from prayer to the Unseen to specific, tangible, concrete results. We believe, deep inside, God's way is our way and God has gotten on board with our will for our lives. We believe our faith and our spiritual discipline will lead us to all those things we want, which we presume God also wants for us.

There are many answers given for this faith dilemma. Some say obedience is what is necessary, in spite of the results. We are to be obedient to what we feel we're asked to do, even if the results may be quite different from what we expected. The call might be a spiritual test to see if we can be obedient and put God first.

Or we might have become confused about what's ultimate in life. We have made our work and our goals ultimate, rather than God. Until we correct our path, we will be like the person worshipping the false idol. It doesn't work.

Or, the problem may not be with God's desire for us, but because we have interrupted the flow from God.

Don't stop the flow

I expect, and there are plenty of Bible verses to suggest, God truly wants to bless us. This doesn't mean God just wants to make us rich, but God's love is ongoing toward us, like a loving Father who wants good things for us, and knows good things include the depth and happiness of being part of the Kingdom. So when our work doesn't go well, clients don't come, the jobs don't pan out as we hoped, we may be the ones who got in the way. It would be much like a water-hose where the water usually flows. When it suddenly stops, we look for the cause. Someone, or something, stepped on the hose. If we're wise, we won't jump to the conclusion that our faith was misplaced, or God was the one who decided to take away, rather than give to us.

There are many ways for us to step on the hose. We might have become entangled with someone in our business who is filling our lives with negative energy and is taking all of our focus and concentration. We might have been going our merry way, and doing our own thing, and gone off track. We may have been confused about what is most important, and found our priorities and our values mixed up. We may have turned out attention away from the Light, and are stuck in the Dark. We have colluded, in some way, with the Dark Side, and it has interrupted the usual flow of our work. And, it may be, there is no clear answer and we won't figure it out.

I have reflected, for some months, on an incident that happened in my business when the flow stopped in the summer of 2007. I had a client who owed me money as a result of canceling a seminar at the last minute after

I had invested in an airline ticket (as was our agreement) and told other potential clients I wasn't available for work for several weeks. The client kept insisting she was a very spiritual person, she always kept her word, and she'd be sending the money owed in two weeks. After two weeks, she promised the money would be sent two weeks later. Then, she changed the timing again. Week after week, month after month, promises were made and not kept. I wondered at what point I should just walk away from this, and how assertive I should be about the money owed. I put into practice a principle I had learned from my career consultant some years before: "When something doesn't work, look at your part in it, and then change the policy." I realized my contract had not been specific enough. I should have had more protections placed in the contract, so if the seminar didn't look as if it would get the needed participants, I could cancel four to six weeks before. I also decided I would never use any of my money toward any seminar in the future (I rarely did this, but made an exception for this very spiritual person, and realized I was wrong to have done so!). I changed the contract for future seminars, but struggled with whether to continue pressuring this person for the money owed.

I noticed my other work began to slow down, and for several weeks, even dried up. But I continued to be diplomatic and assertive, while wondering what was happening to my business. I wondered if God was trying to teach me a lesson. Or if God had pulled the plug for some reason. But in retrospect, I believe becoming embroiled and entangled in the unfulfilled promises and small and large deceptions simply made me turn my attention to the negatives rather than the positives of my business and stopped the flow. I lost sleep over this problem, and kept trying to find creative ways to force this person to come through. If I had to do this over again, I believe I would have given it three tries for the money, changed my policy for the future, considered it an expensive learning experience, recognized this was a test I didn't pass, disengaged from this person, and moved on to put my focus back on what was more important in my business. I would have remembered God has plenty of money and he can more easily give it to me through people who are willing, than through people who are not. *negative focus*

I believe it was my actions that stopped the flow. I was to blame, not God. I began to look at other ways I might be stopping the flow of my work.

I reached the conclusion that sometimes we compromise our work and the corruption we allow ruins the flow. It's as if our work got mucked up, dirtied and sullied, and there's no way it can continue to flow as long as it lacks the purity it once had.

Or we became so embroiled in our work, we forgot what it was all about. We thought our work was about winning the awards and accolades, but it was about giving and being compassionate. We thought it was about becoming wealthy, but we later learned it was about being enriched. We thought it was about doing good deeds, but we learned it was about being a good person. It may be that the whole reason for doing a certain job may have little to do with the results, and more to do with some by-product along the way. We had so much faith in results, we forgot that God's desire for us may be to touch someone with our determination, our courage, or our grace rather than our achievement.

This point became clear to me as I pondered the death of my sister, who I had adored all my life. She died of ALS (Lou Gehrig's disease) in 2006. This is a disease that is, for almost everyone, a clear death knell. Death usually comes about two to three years after the diagnosis, and there is very little anyone can do about it. There are ways to somewhat ease the suffering and there are methods to deal with all the different ways the body begins its decline – inability to swallow, inability to walk, eventually inability to eat except through a feeding tube. My sister, however, was a very religious person and had lived her religion for many years. She tried experimental treatments, her family and church rallied around her, and she did whatever made sense to do. I did, at one point, tell her jokingly I would sacrifice an ox in our backyard if it would cure her, even though it would annoy the neighbors, but we both decided that had little chance of leading to success and wasn't worth the aggravation (even in Colorado, oxen seemed to be in short supply and neighbors don't enjoy the smell!), so we crossed that off our list of possibilities, as well as the idea of going down to a healer in Brazil (who had never cured ALS before!) and flying to Paris for one last hurrah. Eventually, she died. Our prayers for her cure didn't work. She wasn't cured. But she died with great grace and peace.

As I thought about her life and death, I realized one of her greatest gifts to all of us who knew her may have been the grace and surrender and faith by which she accepted what was happening to her. To see someone die well is a blessing for all who witness it. Is it possible the true gift of faith was not what we wanted for her, but the answer to prayer was how she was able to die with little discomfort and pain, with little or no anxiety about death, and with a Spirit that spoke of an authentic relationship with God?

Of course, everything that happens isn't God's will, but it is possible for God to turn events into his will. Sometimes our faith is fulfilled in some unexpected way. We expect our faith to warrant a very specific result. Another result comes our way, and we presume something went wrong. And yes, we may have mis-heard the call. But it may not have gone wrong at all. Our desired result and God's intended result may be quite different.

Becoming risk-takers

If we feel called to do certain work, we are also called to be risk-takers. It doesn't make much sense to commit to an unusual business, or to follow a path few have taken and that seems to have little chance of success. But the call demands of us to take a leap of faith, believing all things are possible if God is part of our lives.

Our leap of faith is a jump into the unknown, without a net, without wires to hold us up, without footprints to follow, and it doesn't come with an instruction book. Everyone, spiritual or not, to some extent, lives by faith, since it's impossible to go through a day without faith in something or someone. But for those who live their lives from a spiritual center, unusual choices often become workable. We may take steps that, to others, may seem foolhardy or simply not getting us anywhere. Or, we may feel led to go to places and do things that seem illogical or even dangerous.

The faithful life is a combination of inward leading and outward action. It is faith and good works. It is our inner love of God expressed in the outer world. As the Book of James says in the New Testament, "Faith without deeds is dead."[35] And works without faith may not be sustainable for any long period of time.

The Catholic theologian Pierre Teilhard de Chardin, who was also a scientist and a palaeontologist, believed the inward Spirit and outward matter were co-existent and can be in unity with each other. He believed that loving God necessarily involved bringing spirituality integrally into our world. Our job is to awaken the spirit in the world in order to allow its influence to grow.[36] It is the spirit within that harmonizes and unifies the inner and the outer. Chardin says: "In all things there is a Within, co-extensive with their Without... God, at his most vitally active and most incarnate is not remote from us, wholly apart from the sphere of the tangible; on the contrary, at every moment he awaits us in the activity, the work to be done, which every moment brings. He is, in a sense, at the point of my pen, my pick, my paint-brush, my needle – and my heart and my thought. It is by carrying to its natural completion the stroke, the line, the stitch I am working on that I shall lay hold on that ultimate end towards which my will at its deepest levels tends... it introduces into our spiritual life a higher principle of unity..."[37]

It is in the combination of the inner and the outer, the passive and the active, the spirit needing the material and the material needing the spirit, that our work and our lives find harmony and unity.

But the way we live our lives is different if faith is part of the equation. In a spiritual life, faith precedes action and action follows faith. You can't have one without the other. C.S. Lewis says about the faith-and-works debate: "It's like asking which blade in a pair of scissors is most important."[38]

Yet many religious people who claim to have faith live their lives *as if* they don't have faith. Faith can become a belief system, rather than an integral part of what moves them into action. They don't trust their leading and hold back from taking those first steps, much less the big leaps. They say they believe and trust, but don't act as if they do. They play it safe, expecting God to do all the work, while they stay quiet and passive and simply pray. They may be called to start a new business, to be a missionary in a far-off place, to work for social justice, but they aren't sure enough about the call to take the first steps. So they wait. And pray. And wait some more. They confess their faith in God, but only if God is a lot clearer and much more aggressive. Otherwise, they'll wait for the big signs, never trusting the small nudges.

There is a saying about "stepping out in faith", and that is what we all do, to some extent. If the nudge is small, we might need to take a baby step to test it. If it's big and clear and loud, we might feel confident enough to buy the plane ticket on faith, to start the business on faith, to invest money in what seems like a risk to others, but is a clear call to us. Of course, there can be a fine line between being cowards and refusing to step out until the call is so loud that even the neighbors hear it. We have to discern when we're simply foolishly hopeful, believing that our desire and God's call might sound the same, even if they aren't the same.

Standing on integrity

In my job within the film industry, I work with both Christian and non-Christian film-makers. I sometimes naively expect those who are Christian to have more faith and more integrity, but this is not always the case. I sometimes see Christians disconnect their faith from their work and rely on their knowledge and experience and even their fears, and leave faith behind.

Perhaps this can best be illustrated by a story. This story combines two different approaches to faith and works which I've noticed many times among Christians in the film industry. This is not based on any one experience, but on a number of people I've observed through the years.

Many times, well-intentioned Christians decide they want to make a film or to have a career in the film industry. They feel called to do this work and believe they can offer something of great value. They sometimes feel called because they've seen many films that have few values and appeal to our baser instincts rather than inspire or uplift. They want to make a difference and have a positive impact. They have ideas about how to do this, and have prayed sincerely and often about this desire. It seems their faith has guided them into the film industry.

Some Christian film-makers rely on their faith but don't back up their faith with their work and preparation. They believe the first draft of their script will become an Academy Award-winning film, even though they've done little to learn the craft of screenwriting, or to prepare for a career in the competitive film industry. They have faith God wants them to make their film and take huge steps in faith to back it up, such as quitting their day job, mortgaging their homes, borrowing against their children's future. They are so sure of themselves but their faith doesn't pan out and it's unclear who really was asking them to take these steps. They have great faith, but no works to back it up.

Others start out having faith that they heard the call and are to proceed. But somewhere along the line, they sometimes lose their faith. No, they don't lose their *belief* in God. They lose their *faith* in God's leading.

When we hear the words, "lose faith", we usually think of someone who has stopped believing in God. But people can just as easily lose their faith by no longer listening. Their faith got them started on their journey, but they don't continue walking by faith. They still believe in God. They still go to church, pray, talk about God. But they stop acting as if God is truly leading them. They figure they know everything about how to get things done, or believe others know everything, and they give others too much power. They begin to trust in themselves and others more than God. They get so caught up in their project, they suffer from spiritual pride, putting themselves above God.

In their zeal to get a film made, integrity falls by the wayside. Faith has started the process, but may not continue day by day. Instead of allowing God's light to shine before them and around them, they turn to the shadows because it seems the shadowy side might get the job done faster. After all, it worked for the non-Christians, so why wouldn't it work for them?

Sometimes many people get manipulated in the process. Out of a zeal and desperation to get the film made, film-makers do foolhardy actions that have no peace around them. They fire the writer, hire another one, fire that one, hire another one. Sometimes this is necessary, but other times it comes out of frenetic activity. They don't trust in the purer process that comes from God. Sometimes film-makers partner up with unethical people, believing the unethical people will have the money or the power or the clout or the knowledge to get the film into production. Sometimes they make foolish decisions, spending all their money to try to get the film into production, even though there is little interest in their script, or little that tells them this is a good idea. Frenetic activity abounds. Sometimes the frenzy makes the producer or writer or director feel very important. After all, he, or she, is in the middle of the exciting whirlwind. Certainly this means things are happening, and they are meant to go forth and make the film. But in the process, when faith and peace get lost, people are wounded, ego comes to the forefront, respect is left behind, and the project begins to topple.

Faith was lost, and so was a film that could have been great. The film-maker put more faith in the people and the project, than faith in God.

At all times, whether our work goes well, or not, we need to take a stand for integrity. The Bible calls this righteousness, meaning to do the right thing, even though it doesn't seem to lead us to where we want to go.

We respect others, even though it might seem they are getting in our way.

We stand up for others, even when other people on our team want to tear them down.

We don't cheat on anything, even though a small cheat seems as if it will make everything go right.

We never put money or fame or power or clout above righteousness, even though temptations abound to push our work off track.

We listen to the leadings, even though it seems we'll make more money if we ignore them.

We try to stay focused on the work, not on money, or fame, or power.

We try to continue to define success in spiritual terms, not the world's terms. We try, through our faith, to find our way, not to lose our way.

Faith needs to stand on integrity, even when all the evidence tells us this makes no sense.

God's strange behavior

Sometimes God seems to be working backwards. Just as we seem to be moving forward toward success, everything can come to a standstill. It might seem God has put a stop to what we thought was his plan.

Danie Ray Hewlett had this experience some years ago when starting her business as a trainer and competitor and riding teacher with reining horses. Reining is the most difficult form of Western Riding, and includes eight difficult maneuvers the horse and rider have to learn. Danie won the International Buckskin World Championship in Open Reining in 2006 and won the International Buckskin World Championship in Open Freestyle in 2006 and 2007.

When she first started her business, she found her faith was tested: "We were struggling. I had gone out on my own as a trainer and teacher, and basically that was a big source of our income. My kids were little, and we were starving along. At that time, I was growing more spiritual, and I had a lot of spiritual battles with a lot of the people that were bringing me horses. They were back-stabbing and nasty and corrupt and I felt they were not morally on the right track. Even though they were coming and paying for me to help them, they were also bad-mouthing me to other people. It seemed as if it was fun for them to play these games. I had a lot of turmoil and the lies they were telling were so bad for my reputation. Finally I prayed, 'God, I just can't fight trying to get better as a trainer. I can't fight trying to raise my kids. I can't fight trying to keep us from starving and do a good job and fight people that are evil, I just can't do it. So, please, take away all who are bad for me and bad spiritually, and please send me good people.' And so my barn left – quite suddenly! Almost every horse was pulled from my barn!

"Here's what happened. This was the year that VS came around – it's related to hoof and mouth disease and people hadn't seen it for a lot of years and it freaked everyone out. It closed down fairs and rodeos that year, and during that time, I had a horse get this so my place was quarantined for thirty days. So the people that had been horrible anyway, after thirty days when they could leave, they flew. I had twelve horses in training at that time and all but two left. But I discovered, ever since I've put my faith in God, I've never done without anything. So even though it took a while to get more horses, I got another job here, got another job there, so something else filled the gap until other horses and owners started coming to my barn. And after that, I only had good people come into my life. I discovered if you want God to command your life, he will, and if you don't, then you get to deal with it all. As a result of this experience, I have never questioned when people don't come to me. I don't ever worry about that."

Creating a vacuum

Sometimes, when we wonder why our business is down, God may have created a vacuum in order for something else to come into our work. It's as if he has to first clean out the house, sweeping the old away, in order to bring in the new. We have to learn to trust this process; otherwise, we'll give up because things don't seem to be going our way.

There is a Bible verse about the person who swept all the demons out of the house and then more came in. The person had created a vacuum, but put nothing else in its place.[39] When a vacuum is created, we can put any number of things in its place while waiting.

Many times in my own life I've seen my work come to a standstill for a period of time. I have learned, over the years, to ask myself, "What am I to do with this vacuum? What should I be putting in its place?" Sometimes I use the time to pray more, or think more. Sometimes I realize I haven't been doing enough of the important non-income-producing activity – whether working more on marketing, coming up with new ideas for a book, doing more volunteer work, or even taking a much-needed vacation.

Sometimes I have wondered if God was joking with me, just to see if I could take a joke.

Several years ago, I reached a dry spell in my business. Instead of the usual two or three scripts (or more) waiting to be read, there was nothing. I prayed for work, and some small jobs would come in. I would thank God for everything that came my way, no matter how small, but sometimes I'd get several calls from potential clients who said they'd send their script the next day, and it never arrived. Sometimes a script would arrive with a check, and the client would immediately call and tell me not to cash the check – they'd had a setback and I needed to send everything back. Sometimes a client would say they wanted an expensive job, and then tell me to do the service that didn't cost as much. Sometimes the script arrived without the check, and the check never came. Day after day, every time something was put in my hands, it seemed to be taken away. I was tempted to manipulate the situation. I'd think, "Quick! Cash the check and tell the person you've already started work and there's no going back!" "Tell the client you'll work on Saturday, even though you know you can't this week!" "Grab hold of the money – do anything for the money, because you need it!" Instead, I simply believed that above all, we stand on integrity. Soon I learned to joke about it with God. "OK, God. Here's a job. Now what will you do with it? Are you being a prankster?" With every setback, I learned to say to God, "Whatever!" I wondered if this was a spiritual test designed to see whether I could put God above money, work, my career. Shortly after that, I sold the proposal for this book, and other work came my way.

I learned, from this experience, to stand on integrity, in spite of all the pushes and nudges and pulls that try to get me off track.

Dr. Douglas Millham from Discover the World, Inc. in Kenya says: "I have become more and more comfortable in the concept of testing God's faithfulness, as God is always testing mine. I assume and accept that God puts me in places to help others, and so as I confront each new situation of need, each new vulnerable child I meet, I challenge myself to find resources to meet the need, commit my heart to see that need through to a good resolution, even as I believe God, in advance, to provide. His Word promises provision, so in reality I'm challenging God, in my own mind and heart, to keep his promises, his faithfulness."

Questions for discussion

1. How do you understand "the leap of faith"? Why is it called a "leap" and not just a "step" of faith?
2. What parts of your career demand faith from you? Do you have faith in your work, or faith in God? How do you understand the difference?
3. When has it been the most difficult to have faith in your career? What are the tests that you've gone through? What were the results?
4. Have you ever had moments when it occurred to you that the results you expected were not the results that were most important spiritually? Discuss what you learned.
5. Are there stories of faith in the Bible that speak to you and have encouraged you when your faith seemed small or insufficient?

Scripture to consider

Go back and read the Old Testament stories of people mentioned in Hebrews 11 – stories told in Genesis chapters 6, 12, 21, 22 and 26. Are there other verses in the Bible about faith that you've memorized, and that have inspired you?

CHAPTER 3

Willing to Be Blessed

All good gifts around us,
are sent from heaven above,
then thank the Lord,
O thank the Lord,
for all his love…

Matthias Claudius[40]

If we only knew how much God would like to bless us! The Bible is filled with verses about blessings – and the many ways God blesses. The land is blessed.[41] Households are blessed.[42] An inheritance is blessed.[43] The crops are blessed.[44] Families and livestock and bread and barns and work are blessed.[45] God blessed with fertility and prosperity and abundance[46] for generations to come. God blessed with peace.[47]

Yes, even Job (eventually) got blessed.

In the New Testament, we're told that just as a father won't give his children stones if they ask for bread, God won't give us bad things, when we ask for the good.[48] And we often believe that all sorts of good things should come our way – comfort, achievement, respect, and a few nice material things along the way.

Yet, considering we're told God wants to bless us, why, then, do we so often feel we are not blessed? Since our work is such an important part of our lives, why do we feel the blessings that should be part of our work elude us? Why is it jobs don't come our way, our businesses don't seem to prosper, we struggle through tough times, money is scarce, and in spite of all our work and preparation, we just scrape by instead of having the abundant, blessed life we were promised? Is this God's fault, or our own? Or might we have missed the boat about what true blessings really are?

The temptation to struggle

In First World developed countries, many believe we achieve success through hard work and through the hard climb to the top. We learn that "If it's worth doing, it's worth doing well!" And doing something well takes time and energy and work. We have heard the saying, "You can do it fast or do it well" and we believe doing it well means a long time of struggle. We presume we'll encounter difficulties and obstacles along the path to success.

So we prepare ourselves for the obstacles and clench our teeth and gird up our loins and go, once more, into the breach. We believe success only comes as a result of scratches and bruises and falling down and getting up again.

We also tend to believe that if we work hard enough and long enough, the blessings of prosperity and a fair amount of wealth and respect will naturally follow – provided, of course, we're willing to make the big effort. We tell ourselves, "I'm such a good person, I deserve success!" And we are shocked if things don't go our way.

In the West, where I live, we're told to "cowboy up" – when you fall off the horse, you cowboy up and climb back on again. And we expect to "cowboy up" again and again and again.

Sometimes all this determination and these many falls build character. Sometimes they only make bruises.

Our temptation to struggle may actually be a hidden desire to prove our determination and self-worth. We believe: The harder the struggle, the better the result. If we show our struggle to the world, the world can easily believe our task is, indeed, difficult, and our work is, indeed, important. The world admires our great perseverance and tremendous commitment to the goal. We become known as the one who never gives up, even when everyone else seems to have fallen by the wayside. When taken to the extreme, there can be an addiction to suffering, and a belief that success only comes from great struggle. Deep down, some of us, in a very subtle way, may take pride in our struggles and difficulties and in the amount of time it takes to do well. There are some hidden pay-offs.

It is possible, for some, there's an obstacle to success that lies with our temptation to struggle, rather than our willingness to be blessed.

Aren't I entitled? Don't I deserve it?

Although many people believe good things take years to achieve, there is another group of people who believe that they're entitled to huge blessings and that good things should come to them with very little effort. They have an expectation of immediate fulfillΔment – a million dollars within the year, a name brand everyone will turn to, respect and power and clout and fame and riches – all coming quickly.

The entitlement group has the opposite expectation of the struggle group. They believe they deserve it, and the minimal amount of work should yield, for them, the maximum amount of success. It is presumed this is how their work will go. After all, if others have good things, certainly they should have good things as well. But when success doesn't come quickly, they give up.

A deeper study of Christian theology tells us a sense of entitlement or a belief that struggles are always essential are not part of a theological mindset. There is little, if anything, in the Bible about deserving. God is great. God is good. What is ours in life comes from God's goodness and love, not from our deserving. If we think success will come our way because we're just a little bit nicer than the other guy, it's not going to happen! Anyway, not for that reason.

This doesn't mean we're bad people and we should go into a depressive funk over our low self-esteem. Theologically, it simply means we are not little gods, able to command the minions to bow to us and give us their business.

Those who are tempted to struggle may struggle too long. Those who believe they're entitled may not be willing to struggle at all. For both, the obstacles to success may be coming from their side, not God's.

The suspension of disbelief

There is a term we sometimes use in drama called "the suspension of disbelief". When audiences come to the theater, they sit in their comfortable seats and watch characters in a play. They know they aren't really in someone's living room or bedroom, or really watching a murder take place, or really watching people falling in love. They suspend their disbelief and pretend all of this is true in order to enter into the story.

When audiences come to the movie theater, they also suspend their disbelief. They know they aren't really flying in a spaceship to another galaxy, or really watching the end of the world, or really watching the team win the championship. It's all pretend. They don't believe this is all real life. But the audience suspends their disbelief in order to enjoy the film.

When we begin a new job, we also suspend our disbelief. A part of us doesn't know for sure, and may not even believe, this job will go well. We might wonder if we'll like our colleagues and clients and if they'll like us, or if we'll do well, or if we'll find all sorts of problems we couldn't predict. But, we suspend our disbelief to give ourselves fully to the work, and to try to do the best we can, believing in the possibility of success.

The ability to suspend our disbelief is one of the first steps to learn to accept blessings. We need to suspend our disbelief that we could possibly be blessed, and instead, we need to believe in the possibility of being blessed. Maybe we won't be blessed, but maybe we will be richly blessed, far more than we expect.

The success prayer

Before I started my business in 1981, I struggled with the "whys" about success. Why weren't things going my way, in spite of preparation, experience, and willingness? I looked at all aspects of my life and even analyzed myself in case there were glaring faults within me or inappropriate behavior. I came to the conclusion that I didn't dress funny. I was a reasonably nice person without any serious mental illness or character flaws. I had spent years studying drama – certainly I had something to contribute. Why, then, did success seem so far away?

It's easy to believe the obstacles come from God's side. We can blame God for our lack of success. If we're prepared, is God withholding? Might it be we're off-center? Perhaps we're not praying enough, or are forgetting to "seek first his kingdom and his righteousness, and all these things will be given to you as well."[49] Maybe we're seeking in the wrong direction.

But what if the obstacles are actually coming from our side? If God wants to bless us, and we're not receiving blessings, might it be that we're putting up the barriers, not God? Might it be that our fear of success, or our horror at becoming the greedy types often associated with success, or our unwillingness to do what is necessary, are really the problem? Are we more afraid of success than we are of failure? Is it possible there's something in our own attitudes that is getting in our way?

After many years of small, dead-end jobs, and no sense my career was taking off, I began to wonder if the problems came from me, and if I needed help in resolving these problems. I finally said a prayer I later called "The Success Prayer":

> God, I'm thinking I'm creating the obstacles.
> If so, I pray you would help me do
> whatever is needed to remove them.

Recognizing this may take courage, I prayed for courage. Recognizing this may take help from others, I prayed for help:

> I'm willing to look at whatever is necessary within myself.
> If I need courage to look at these barriers,
> Then give me courage.
> If I need help, then send me help.
> I'm willing to do whatever is necessary to break down the barriers
> between me and success.
> If I need a therapist to help,
> Then I pray you send me a good one (who's also cheap!).

I recognized it may not be in God's best interest to bless me if I lost touch with God. So I added a "Promise Prayer":

> God, considering my relationship with you
> for the past years has been one of getting by,
> of dealing with my anxiety,
> of praying you get me through one more day,
> I realize success will change our relationship.
> If so, I promise I won't desert you.
> I will continue to pray, worship, and read the Bible.
> I will have faith our relationship won't be lost,
> But will change to something even better!

After fourteen years of living on the edge, success came within a year. And the cheap therapist? I found an excellent psychology student at the Jung Center in Los Angeles who worked with me for several years on a sliding scale. She was cheap, but good. I was also doubly blessed with a career consultant who just happened to also write scripts and was willing to trade services.

Are we willing? *to be blessed with success?*

There can be many reasons why we aren't willing to be blessed: Because of an unhappy childhood that makes us believe we don't deserve good things. Because of our unwillingness to dream big. Because we're not willing to do the preparation necessary for the job we want or we lack the knowledge to get the goal. Because what we want will get in the way of our relationship with God, rather than nurture our relationship.

Sometimes, we push away blessings because our theology doesn't allow us to have them. We see God as someone more willing to take away than to give.

Most of us grow up with two theologies that sometimes fight against each other. The one theology comes from Original Sin. The other comes from Original Blessings.

The Original Sin theology comes from Genesis 1 and 2. Adam and Eve began their blessed lives in the Garden of Eden. Everything was in harmony. They were told to care for and cultivate the Garden and they did. Plants grew. Animals lived in harmony with them. Even Adam and Eve, and God, got along just fine.

With the Sin of grabbing for what wasn't theirs, they were cursed. And the curse in every aspect of their life brought disharmony. Adam was told the work of his hands would no longer easily give him crops. Eve was told she would have pain in childbearing. Even the serpent was cursed. All were exiled from the harmony of the Garden.

With Original Sin theology, we believe we are forever cursed, which also means our relationships and our work are intrinsically cursed. We believe it is in the nature of life that things will be difficult, we won't get what we want, and blessings will forever elude us. We aren't in harmony, because of the disobedience of those two people in the Garden.

We remember the otherwise comforting song, "Amazing Grace", which tells us we are wretches. We might remember reading about Jonathan Edwards, who wrote we are "sinners in the hands of an angry God!"[50] Others tell us God is a God of revenge. We feel hated, not loved.

We forget that Christian theology says that Christ has redeemed us, and redeemed the world and moved us, potentially, back into harmony.

Yet, if we're to be blessed, we need to fit the idea of blessings into our theological mindset. To do this, we might look to another biblical theology.

The theology of blessing

St. Julian of Norwich (1342–1416) said, "I know well that heaven and earth and all creation is great, generous and beautiful and good… God's goodness fills all his creatures and all his blessed works full, and endlessly overflows in them."[51] She saw the whole creation was blessed at its very center.

Blessing is a word of considerable power. The first chapter of Genesis tells the story of the Creation. Again and again we are told "... and God saw that it was good." It is possible to argue that this is the unfallen condition of the world: that of living in a natural state of blessing.[52] Blessing is to be given, and received: one does not bless without investing something of oneself into the receiver of one's blessings. Can one truly receive blessing if one is ignorant of the gracious giver? If it is true that all creation flows from a single, loving source, then surely all of creation is blessed, and is itself a blessing.[53]

The power of blessings is "not the power of control or the power of being over or being under, but the power of fertility." Blessing makes things bigger. It expands. It is a sign of fertility, of great grace, of extravagance.[54] It is an image of overflowing, of great pleasure, of great gifts – a banquet of abundance.[55] Many Bible verses about blessing use words like "flourishing",[56] or say that all our undertakings and labors are blessed,[57] or speak about receiving peace and prosperity.[58] There is a sense of overflowing and abundance.

Blessings are reciprocal. We bless others, we bless God, and as the Psalmist says, "May these reflections of mine give him [God] pleasure as much as Yahweh gives me!"[59] We ask for blessings for us and for the next generation, and if we experience the blessings, we lose our sense of being deprived, and our ever-widening empty spiral of acquisition. We don't have to get and get some more, because we are blessed, first and foremost, and it is the most basic of God's gift to us. It predates sin and it is what our relationship with God was meant to be.

The Old Testament scholar Walter Brueggemann says he sees blessing as "the capacity to transmit energy and power for life from one to another. When God blessed creation, it became fruitful in Genesis 1. Human persons can give blessings as in Genesis 27. Equally interesting is the summons of Psalm 103:1–2, 20–22 which must mean more than praise." He sees blessings as circular, "but not just 'back again', but out beyond to others." He says, "I think blessings move in concentric circles rather than a closed circle."

The German theologian Claus Westermann says most blessings mentioned in the Bible involve salvation and deliverance, and are not just horizontal but also vertical.

If we believe blessings are just about getting good things, we have missed the boat. It is not enough to just get good things so we can become better consumers and be more respected and live a more comfortable life. Of course, we see plenty of evidence of people who seem to be blessed – with the things of the world – but since it is God who gives blessings which sustain us, if we're closed to God, and not in a relationship with God, we're missing the vertical part of the blessing – the part that goes far beyond having nice things. The vertical dimension includes the things of the Spirit that enter into the good things – a greater awareness of God's love for us, of peace, fulfillment, empowerment to do good for others, and the multiplication of our gifts.

These blessings go far beyond "Have a good day!" and "Hope all goes well with the job!" They add another layer to a fulfilling career. Westermann lists some of these blessings: "growth, success, increase, provision."[60] While discussing blessing, he summarizes ideas from a variety of other theologians, including Ludwig Kohler and Johannes Pedersen, saying, "the act of blessing…

means imparting vital power to another person. The one who blesses gives the other person something of his own soul."[61] So blessing must be reciprocal. "The soul is a totality, filled with power. This power lets the soul grow and prosper so it can maintain itself and do its work in the world. This vital power, without which no living being can exist, the Israelites called *berakhah*, 'blessing'. Blessing is both internal and external – the inner power of the soul and the good fortune that produces that power… blessing is vitality. The one who possesses blessing is *barukh*, full of *berakhah*. Power must flow out from him in every direction… blessing is reciprocal."[62] So blessing has a relationship with "growth, maturity, prosperity, and the bearing of fruit, in other words, to well-being."[63]

Blessing is not just about entering into a more comfortable life on earth, but about entering into the Kingdom.[64] Since the Kingdom is broad and wide and eternal, there are no boundaries to blessings. They are meant to keep rippling out, causing things to mature and grow and prosper and make everything bigger than it would be without the work of God.

The Irish teacher and poet, John O'Donohue, in his book *To Bless the Space Between Us*, draws on Celtic spirituality to look at the meaning of blessings. He says, "when you bless someone, you literally call the force of their infinite self into action."[65]

Our work doesn't prosper just for us – it prospers others. If we think it's just for us, so we can brag about how much God has blessed us with riches, we have misinterpreted the difference between material gain and true blessings. If there is no ripple effect, we haven't truly been blessed. We are blessed, and therefore we can bless others. O'Donohue says: "When you bless another, you first gather yourself; you reach below your surface mind and personality, down to the deeper source within you – namely, the soul. Blessing is from soul to soul. And the key to who you are is your soul."[66]

If there isn't an inner transformation within us as a result of the good that has come our way, we have only received the horizontal part of the blessing and missed the connection with the Holy Spirit. So, as we bless others, it also means "to invoke divine favor upon them." As O'Donohue explains, "a blessing is different from a greeting, a hug, a salute, or an affirmation; it opens a different door in human encounter… it awakens future wholeness."[67]

This means we need to put our work into a larger context, recognizing that to be blessed in our work means to make things grow within and without. I want my work to ripple outward and to bless others, and for their work to bless others also. Our work needs to build up the Kingdom, even in ways we can't begin to understand or recognize.

In sports, we might hear "Keep it moving! Don't hold onto the ball – get it into someone else's hands!" Nothing happens when something or someone is fenced in. We need to open the gates and get the blessings circulating as they come to us and then go out again.

In the play *The Matchmaker* and the film *Hello, Dolly*, the main character, Dolly, says, "Money should be like manure. It should be spread around, helping things grow." Same with blessings. We take them in. We allow them to pull us into the world of gratitude and well-being and peace, and then we push them out again, into the lives of others. We recognize what blessings are made for – to build up the Kingdom! And we begin to recognize the power of our work to bless our joy and good health and sense of well-being, but also to bless the work of others. Westermann says, "Blessing involves God's friendly approach to those who will receive him."[68] And our friendly approach to others.

Non-attachment to blessings

If Matthew Fox is right, God wants to bless us (and there is plenty of evidence in the Bible for this theology), so we need to hold our hands open for these blessings and accept them – in whatever surprising form they come to us. However, there's a catch: Whatever gets in the way of our relationship with God is not a blessing. Whatever serves and expands this relationship – is.

We can become attached to these blessings, and get confused about what is most important. We can begin to feel so good about business coming our way, the promotion and raise, the things that come with success, that we can begin to worship the things of the world, rather than serve the Spirit. We can become so attached, we cling to material things rather than find freedom in spiritual things. We might begin to think all of these good material things came from our efforts, and take credit for everything good that happens to us.

Eastern religions (such as Buddhism) train their practitioners to learn to detach from the things of the world. This spiritual training sometimes comes by asking monks to have very few possessions in their lives (a monk's robe and a bowl for rice, perhaps), or by doing menial tasks such as cleaning city streets or toilets. This spiritual training is meant to put their minds on the things of the Spirit, not the things of the world.

The Christian religion seems more focused on non-attachment rather than detachment. In many ways, Christianity is a rather materialistic religion. Not that it worships material things, but it is a religion of involvement in the world. There is an emphasis on God's creation which means, for many of us, loving the earth and being good stewards of it. We are told to use our spiritual gifts in our work. We are told to go out among the people of the world – whether they are poor or rich, sick or healthy. We are to be "in the world but not of the world."[69] We are to engage.

Yet, we are also told to put our focus on the things of the Spirit. We can enjoy prosperity, but we can get along without it. We can enjoy success in the world's terms, yet we are not to make it ultimate. We can be wise with our material blessings, while recognizing that the most important blessings are the gifts of the Spirit – love, joy, peace, patience, kindness, goodness, trustfulness, gentleness and self-control.[70] We are to be psychologically and spiritually free of the things of the world, but not necessarily to reject them. We can enjoy them, live with them, appreciate them, but we can do without them because they aren't ultimate.

If the relationship with God is the most important relationship, then our work serves that relationship. Rather than clinging to results, or our expectations of how we believe our life should unfold, we let go instead. We don't attach. That doesn't mean we don't enjoy good things in life when they come to us. But we don't need them and they are not ultimate. We can live without them if need be. We can enjoy them if they're given to us. And we learn how to keep them moving outward.

This is not an easy place to get to. Our world – especially those of us who live in developed First World countries – is run by materialism. We depend on our machines and our technology and our luxuries. We're told to spend more in order to be good consumers. We don't define success at all by getting by. We define it by how much we have.

My career consultant once told me not to define success by money. That is only one indicator and sometimes not the best one. Define it, instead, by the increase in opportunities you have, the good you do, the positive response of your clients.

My mother once told me, "If the only thing in life you don't have is money, you're way ahead of everyone else!"

Accepting blessings

Sometimes we might wonder if a blessing is really a temptation. Something good is put in front of us. It's something we've always wanted. We wonder if God is teasing us, or testing us, or if it really could be ours. We might wonder if it's a temptation and we're supposed to say "no". Or, we might wonder if it's a true blessing and our response is to hold out our hands, and give praise and thanks to God.

In 2001, I had an opportunity to fulfill a long-term dream – to live in the mountains of Colorado. Although my husband and I had talked, often, about moving out of Los Angeles and living somewhere else, and although I knew the area around Colorado and felt both of us could make it in our careers being outside Los Angeles, we always thought of this dream as far off into the future. I had fallen in love with Colorado when I first vacationed here at the age of thirteen. I went to college in Colorado Springs and loved the land in a way I hadn't experienced before. During a visit to Colorado in 2001, I decided to look at real estate – just for fun. The realtor showed me a beautiful log home which was more than I could ever have imagined. I wondered, "Is this a temptation or a blessing? Can we do this? Am I risking my career by moving? But what if God truly is trying to bless me? What if I said 'yes' to the blessing, instead of 'no'? Is it possible one of my greatest dreams could be fulfilled, and my business could still continue to prosper?"

After much thought and prayer and contemplation, my husband and I decided it would not be foolhardy and willful for us to say "yes". We moved to our new home and immediately named it "Mountain Blessings"!

We can learn about how to accept blessings by looking at the two Magnificats in the Bible – the Magnificat of Hannah in the Hebrew Scriptures and the Magnificat of Mary in the New Testament.

When Hannah, who was barren, had been taunted and provoked by others because she had no children, she prayed to God, crying out: "O LORD Almighty, if you will only look upon your servant's misery and remember me, and not forget your servant but give her a son, then I will give him to the LORD for all the days of his life…"[71]

When Hannah presented her son, Samuel, to the Temple, she then prayed and worshiped God, saying:

> My heart exults in Yahweh,
> In my God is my strength lifted up,
> My mouth derides my foes,
> For I rejoice in your deliverance.

There is no Holy One like Yahweh…
No Rock like our God…
For Yahweh is a wise God,
His to weigh up deeds.
The bows of the mighty have been broken
But those who were tottering are now braced with
strength…
Yahweh gives death and life…
Yahweh makes poor and rich,
He humbles and also exalts.
He raises the poor from the dust,
He lifts the needy from the dunghill
To give them a place with princes,
To assign them a seat of honor,
For to Yahweh belong the pillars of the earth,
On these he has poised the world.
He safeguards the steps of his faithful
But the wicked vanish in darkness
(for human strength can win no victories)…
Yahweh judges the ends of the earth,
He endows his king with power,
He raises up the strength of his Anointed.

1 Samuel 2:1–10 (NJB)

Whereas Hannah asked for the blessing, Mary did not. She was chosen to be richly blessed by carrying the child of God. After her initial shock, she first thanked God for the blessing, and then accepted it. Mary said:

My soul proclaims the greatness of the Lord,
And my spirit rejoices in God my Savior,
Because he has looked upon the humiliation of his
servant.

Yes, from now onwards all generations will call
me blessed,
For the Almighty has done great things for me.
Holy is his name,
And his faithful love extends age after age to those
who fear him.
He has used the power of his arm,
He has routed the arrogant of heart.
He has pulled down princes from their thrones
and raised high the lowly,
He has filled the starving with good things, sent
the rich away empty.
He has come to the help of Israel his servant,
mindful of his faithful love –
according to the promise he made to our ancestors
of his mercy to Abraham and to his descendants
for ever.

Luke 1:46–55

Although the blessings offered to them were beyond their
comprehension, they didn't push them away nor did
they accept them as if it was their due. They surrendered
themselves to God's will, praised God, thanked God,
realized the importance of humility, and recognized the
source of the blessing. They accepted a greater destiny
than they could ever have envisioned for themselves.

Willing to live in the land of plenty

Although it seems strange anyone would push away
blessings, we often do. We can't believe they're meant
for us. We're not sure about accepting so much goodness.

And we worry about ourselves – who will we become if we dwell too long in the Land of Plenty?

The Singapore businessmen Ken Swee and Alex Lo both are Christian business owners, and both were concerned about this problem when they began their businesses. Ken says: "I remember being headhunted to Smith Barney from the Government for one and a half years and one of the things which I hesitated about before I took this job was – what if I would forget God when I had plenty? I knew being in this job, pay would have gone up and it is not unheard of for brokers and advisors to make good money. A dear Christian Grandfather in Perth called Mr. Pitman reassured me: 'If God will give you money, it is because he knows you can handle it.' When I started out, money did not come. I was one of the few investment advisors taking public transport and feeling very hard on the pockets. I thank the Lord because he didn't make it easy as I would not have valued money if it came easy. In fact, it was a hard two years. I remember going to God one day, asking him if it was truly that he led me to this place, and I really felt I couldn't make it and on that day, the Lord provided my biggest client through a cold call. He was a Christian who called me. As I looked back, God was trying to teach me dependence on him. He is the provider, after all."

Alex Lo had similar questions and hesitancies: "In the 1990s, I was a part of a Christian group led by Mr. Chuck Broughton named the 4Cs Program, short for Calling, Clarification, Career, Conviction. A passage we studied was about 'living in plenty' from Philippians 4. I was uneasy as I heard God telling me he will give me plenty. My issue then was what will become of me when he did that. Will I become proud? Self-sufficient? Forget about God? In the passage, Paul says, "I know what it is to be in need, and I know what it is to have plenty. I have learned the secret of being content in any and every situation, whether well fed or hungry, whether living in plenty or in want. I can do everything through him who gives me strength."[72]

Turning our curses into blessings

If we're realistic, we also understand that sometimes things seem to be cursed. We are cursed with bad health and aren't able to do the work we want to do. We are cursed with all sorts of things going wrong at the same time: We get ill. Our house burns down. The stock-market crashes. Our spouse leaves us. Our kids are on drugs. We're the victim of a violent crime that shatters our world. It seems as if we're like Job – our life truly is cursed.

Christian hope recognizes that at the center of all things, there is a blessing. Creation isn't evil, but has been proclaimed good.[73] God brings order out of chaos, goodness out of evil, and can turn curses into blessings.

We can see this in the many stories of forgiveness and redemption. The victims of violent crimes form organizations that try to better the world for others. Elizabeth Eliot's husband and other missionaries were killed in Ecuador, and out of this tragedy, Elizabeth and the families of the others continued to work with the Auca Indians. Their story is told in two films – *The End of the Spear* and *Beyond the Gates*.

The Amish practised forgiveness for the family of the killer of their schoolchildren, and showed the world how a spiritual community can transform tragedy.

We turn our curses into blessings when we continue to make something good out of the downturns that come our way. This might mean trying to learn a spiritual lesson from the problems we face. Or learning to depend more on God when things don't go our way. Or changing a business practice when things seem to go against us and it's clear our present way of working isn't being effective. Or, it might simply mean we don't lose the calling to be good and do good in spite of the forces against us.

Pass it on

We are also told to do something in our work that may seem counter-intuitive. We are told to be good to those who curse us, and to pass on our blessings to others. God told Abraham, "I will bless those who bless you,"[74] and in Numbers, Balak says, "I know that those you bless are blessed."[75] We're told to pass on our blessings, and to bless others – including blessing our enemies.[76]

Most of us work in competitive businesses. There's room for only one at the top. There is competition from others for the business we offer. There are many people vying for the same piece of the pie. Why would we share our blessings with others, when it will only cut into our own profits?

Why? Because we live in a world of abundance, not scarcity. Blessings are at the very core of our lives and at the center of our world. We grease the wheels of the world with generosity. We assure a future when we teach, mentor, and nurture the next generation. We create a better earth when our product improves lives. We pass

111

it on and become givers, rather than takers, because there truly is enough to go around.

Alex Lo says, "God blesses us that we can be His channels of blessings. I am reminded of the parable in Matthew 25. More will be required of him who has been blessed with more. Hence, my responsibility is to use whatever he has blessed me with to bless others."

The film *Pay it Forward* showed how blessings can continue to grow and ripple outward. We are to keep it moving. Or, as some say, "What goes around, comes around!"

We are to bless, support, care for, and sometimes even encourage our competition.

We are to do our work in a way that blesses others, blesses our world, expands the Kingdom, and recognizes that our work can be a source for the blessings of others.

O'Donohue gives a blessing for work:

> May you see in what you do the beauty of your soul.
> May the sacredness of your work bring light and renewal
> to those who work with you
> and to those who see and receive your work.
> May your work never exhaust you.
> May it release wellsprings of refreshment,
> Inspiration, and excitement...
> May your soul calm, console, and renew you.[77]

Questions for reflection and discussion

1. Before you read this chapter, how did you define blessing? Has your definition changed in any way?

How do you differentiate between horizontal and vertical blessings?

2. When have you been especially blessed? In what way did this blessing bring you closer to God?

3. How have you blessed others? Have you ever watched the reciprocal effect of blessing? Have you ever watched your blessing going outward, to more and more people?

4. Is there anything that holds you back from blessing others in your work? Perhaps a sense of competition? A feeling that someone else might get what you want?

5. What blessings would you like to have in your life? Would you recognize them if they came to you? In what way could these blessings bring you peace? Joy? Good will? Health?

Scripture to consider

Read some of the verses about blessings: Genesis 12:2–3; 26:3, 24; 27:29, 34, 38; Deuteronomy 28:8, 12; 1 Chronicles 4:10; Psalm 109:28; Luke 6:28; Romans 12:14; Hebrews 6:14.

CHAPTER 4

Becoming Important

When you're tempted to think you're so important,
remember visions of you have probably not been
seen in Bolivia!

My friend, Cathleen Loeser

Success, like failure, brings with it extra baggage. Sometimes that baggage is like a suitcase filled with wonderful things – new adventures, additional opportunities, pretty new possessions, exciting relationships. But not always. And sometimes our fear of the negatives of success may keep us from becoming successful.

Many of us might be happy to have some extra fortune, but would not choose extra fame. How many of us really want to be a Tom Cruise, or Queen Elizabeth, or Billy Graham, or the president or prime minister of our country, recognized by most people and guarded, protected, and sometimes threatened?

Some of us might wonder if we were better known, with more power and clout, if this would ruin us. If we become more famous, instead of gaining meaning, we may lose it. We may lose simplicity, clarity, and be pushed around by everyone else's idea of who we should be.

What would happen to us if we became a more public figure? Our particular public may vary in numbers. The president or vice-president of a company, whether large or small, may only be known to a few people. Politicians and their families, musicians, writers, actors, astronauts, scientists, may be known locally, nationally, or worldwide.

With importance, we move from being a private person, known only to people we've met, and become a public person, where everyone who has heard of us has an opinion of us – right or wrong.

Becoming a public person

In almost all forms of success, we move from being a private person, secure in our home and our family, to becoming a public person, known by the larger world. Many cultures and religions say a woman's place is in the home and the man's place is in the public square. Although this is changing in many cultures, as women become more public figures, we still carry remnants of this thinking. Often the woman still sweeps the floors and the man takes out the garbage, connecting with the larger world. The woman makes the bed, the man washes the car in the driveway. The woman prepares the children for the larger world. The man takes them into the world, and makes policies or votes for policies that will help their journey.

But being a male, or female, doesn't necessarily mean the person is more private, or public. Our success and increased visibility is often what pushes a person into the public square.

As most of us do better in our jobs, others seek our opinion, and others have opinions about our opinions. We begin to have more influence on policies that are made in our companies. As a small-business owner, we may be asked to serve on a board, or to join a group of others in our field, or to speak up about policies that might affect our work.

For many of us, we'd rather just do our job and be comfortable and safe. Speaking out can get us into trouble. Many times, we decide to stay in a less influential place, even though we may feel called to be influential. We fear the extra responsibilities and the possibility that we may say the wrong thing, lose friends and alienate colleagues, and have extra pressures we don't want, didn't ask for, and feel we don't need. As a result, we may be the biggest barrier to our greater success.

Overcoming the barriers to importance

When I had been a failure long enough, and wondered if I would ever find any form of success, I thought about the barriers to my success. I realized if I were successful, people might envy me and even dislike me. I realized I wanted to be liked more than I wanted to be successful. As I thought further about it, I recognized I had little control over what people thought of me, especially those who had never met me. I decided to make some more promises to God and to try to break through this barrier. I told God:

> If you help with my success, I will try not to misuse the power that comes with it. I'll try not to give anyone a good reason not to like me. I will try to be encouraging and supportive of others, as I would like them to be encouraging and supportive of me. I will try to be helpful of others who are seeking success whenever possible. I will try to exhibit

in my relationships the fruits of the Spirit,
not the usual fruits of competition. Although
I recognize there will be some people who
misinterpret me, I will try not to be the reason
for that interpretation.

In all my prayers about success, I tried to affirm the
partnership I wanted with God.

As my business began to grow, I began to recognize
some of the other baggage of success.

Everyone wants a piece of you

The more successful one becomes, in many cases, the
more other people want to partner up with success. For
every presidential candidate, there are those who want
to be the vice-president, because it takes less work, less
campaigning, but still lets the politician rub elbows
closely with the top guy. For every rock musician, there
are the groupies who want to be close and touch the
electricity of fame. For every successful person, there
are those who want to be known as their friend, their
colleague. They want other people to know how close
they are to this Very Important Person.

People want to know all the juicy gossip about
successful people. They want to know about their
private lives, not just about their public opinions. And if
they don't know the details and the particulars about the
latest gossip, they often make them up.

After I became somewhat of a celebrity within my
own world of screenwriting, one of the members of our
Quaker Meeting in Santa Monica asked me one day,

"Are you kind of a star?"

I laughed, and said, "Well, within my own small world, I'm fairly well known. But why do you ask that question?"

Colleen replied, "I was talking to someone and your name came up. They became very excited when I mentioned you were a friend of mine, and you were a member of Santa Monica Friends Meeting. Suddenly the person started asking me many questions – about what you were like, who you were married to, and other personal questions. A little red flag went up in my mind, and I simply replied, 'She's very nice!'"

I told Colleen that was the right response. After that, I learned that people who didn't know me but knew about me were discussing me when hiking with friends, on trains, in conferences, in offices, in restaurants. Sometimes I got emails from people I didn't know. Although much of it was positive, some of it was hate mail where the person clearly knew little about who I was.

As my friend Cathleen reminded me, "That all comes with being a public figure!" And then she would add, nicely, "You'll have to learn to deal with it if this is the career you want!"

When I multiplied my experiences a thousand times, to gain insights into people who were far more important than me, I could see the problems quite clearly. Being important means many extra stresses – VIPs are asked for interviews, to be on the Board or contribute to charities, to be spokespersons at events, to write books and give speeches and to share their star power with others. They are asked to do more and more but find the more they do for others, the more they might lose themselves and their own personal goals.

Some might say, "I want none of that! Just give me a little job I can do well, day by day!" But if we are called to share our talents, and if that calling includes becoming important, then the choice of saying "no" is not a choice at all. Of course we're going to say "yes" to the reasonable demands that allow us to do more good. But we have to find a way around the problem of importance.

Becoming the object of resentment

With success also comes jealousy. Others see the accolades we get, the respect and admiration we receive, and become resentful of us. One of my interview subjects said, "Success can come at a great price!" Several people I interviewed recounted examples of attacks from others, misinterpretations, colleagues who refused to talk to the person, jealousy and the inability to have a civil conversation with those who hated their success.

Novelist Jerry Jenkins, the author of over 175 books (including the best-selling *Left Behind* series which he wrote for Tim LaHaye), recognizes that jealousy and various inaccurate opinions come with the territory of success. He says, "I was once interviewed by a local reporter who asked, 'What's this rumor about your using your newfound wealth to update a bathroom for six figures?' This was ludicrous, but how do you prove a negative? So no yachts or homes on the continent or our own jet for us. And certainly no six-figure bathroom. You can't control what people think or say, but when they come to conclusions opposite of your intentions, it's frustrating."

Yet, there can be ways to handle resentment from

others. It's possible to be diplomatic, even to people who hate us. It's possible to be supportive of those who resent our success, and help them become successful. It's possible to do good, even to those who seem to stand in our way, and to remove them from our path with kindness, rather than with hatred.

Losing our perspective

Many embrace being important, because it often means more clout and more money. But this can lead to pride and egos that no longer care much for others, who we believe are beneath us. We lose our relationships in the process and can become classist, or snobbish, or simply elitist.

I decided to explore this issue of being important by talking to some people whose names I had heard for a number of years and who I knew were Very Important People, either nationally or within their particular field.

Dr. Martin Marty is one of the foremost church historians and theologians of our day. He's written over 50 books, contributed to over 5,000 articles, spoken to thousands of people. I first heard of him when I was in seminary in the 1970s. Since then, his name often comes up in theological or Christian circles and when his name is mentioned, it's said with great respect. It's clear to me that within his area of Christianity, Dr. Marty, now at the age of eighty, is a Very Important Person.

He discussed the various problems that come with success and ways to overcome them: "One of the difficulties of being important is the loss of perspective. You think you're important, but you may not be as important to others as you think you are. I once read that Joseph Brodsky, a Nobel prize winning poet, said, 'All right, I had the Nobel Prize, which would be considered important, but in any city in the world, for any person who would know who I am, there would be a thousand who wouldn't.' That's what you have to keep remembering. There were times I'd walk down the street in Chicago with Saul Bellow, who was one of the best-known novelists of our time, and nobody would say, 'Hi, Saul' even though we were in his own city. Who would know him in Cape Town or in Moscow? This world is so complex, that however much of a niche you might have, most people could pass you right by."

Actor and director Denzel Washington also recognizes that perspective is important. Before he begins to do any work, he says the work is already "prayer-filled". As he explains, "Spirituality doesn't play a role in my life; it *is* my life. Everything else is just making a living. If I get away from that idea, I get lost. The business is not who I am. Anyone with a spiritual base understands humility. When you start using the words 'I' and 'me' too often, you get in trouble."[78]

Jerry Jenkins also recognizes the importance of keeping perspective: "This is an important issue, which can be even more dangerous than the temptations that come with failure. Too often, failure leads to clearer, more easily learned lessons. Needless to say, despite how one might feel about himself and his success, you never reach a place where spiritual disciplines – church, being in the Bible, prayer, sharing your faith – become less important. In fact, they become more important to assure you remember who you are (the same flawed person you've always been) and who you're not (God)."

Jerry adds: "In many ways I'm grateful that my

visibility – because the bottom line is that this is all that is – came in my forties rather than when I was younger, because it may have turned my head. By the time your kids are almost grown, you know yourself fairly well and realize nothing has changed except that: visibility. People tend to put you on a pedestal, make both positive and negative assumptions about you that have no basis in reality, laugh louder at your jokes, etc. The biggest temptation is wanting to be to them what they think you are, some super-spiritual saint. At the end of some very public days, all I want to do is quit smiling."

It is tempting to concur with others' sense of our importance. But importance becomes a test of perception and humility. Others might think we're some sort of gods, but it's our job to put them back into reality. We are not the gods of our careers. We are servants. We do our work because we love it, we feel called to it, and we contribute something good to life by doing it. When I've trained script consultants, I usually tell them, "When people tell you, 'You're the best there is!' a good answer is, 'I'm glad I can be of help!'" Others might lose their perspective, but we're asked to keep ours.

Forgetting our roots

Dr. Marty says, "When we become important, we might also forget our roots, which means losing part of our identity. If you don't have roots, that's one brand of the problem, but if you have roots, forgetting them is another. I'm a Nebraska kid, raised with the drought and depression and Dust Bowl and all the rest, and yet I was nurtured by people who got us reading, got us curious about the world, gave us love. In my case, my father was a church organist and taught me composers like Bach. I've collected Great Plains novels, such as those of Willa Cather and Wright Morris. In your imagination, these become reference points.

"Some years ago I was asked to give a Governor's lecture at the University of Nebraska and then at the University of Illinois. I took the lines from Santayana, 'Everyone needs a place to stand to view the world.' Santayana had two reference points – Spain and Harvard. My two are Nebraska and the University of Chicago. By which I mean, I shuttle forth between them.

"I try keep the values from those reference points of the heart, learned from those people who endured everything and yet are generous. So there's something you always try to keep from the dimensions of childhood. I like to keep a dual perspective in proportion – of the provincial and the cosmopolitan."

Keep old friends

Dr. Marty recognized there are other hazards to celebrity – such as losing friendships: "Celebrities do not have friends, they have claques. Nobody can go up to a celebrity and give them a perspective. Paparazzi might follow them, they have PR agents, but they don't have friends. But we need friends, people who can say, 'Marty, that time you went too far.'"

Dr. Marty also suggested that we should have relationships where we can confess to another: "I'm an ordained minister and sometimes people come to me and formally confess. I give them absolution and the sacrament after it. They tell me horrendous things and their names will go to the grave with me. I wish some of the celebrities were in that kind of relationship instead of only hearing applause."

Many spiritual people make sure they always have friends who will tell them the truth. It's easy to believe the good opinions of others, especially when there is a constant refrain of what fabulous, splendid, terrific people we are. We can be tempted to believe that's the whole truth and nothing but the truth. But the truth is, we are far more than that, and if we forget our sins, our imperfections, we also forget our need for balance and our need for God.

Some of us make sure our friends know their very important role in our lives: their job is to always tell us the truth. And we choose these friends for their wisdom, their insight, and their inability to be intimidated by fame.

When I started to do well in my business, I realized others may not tell me the truth. I also realized it was not always good business to tell everyone about my foibles. If people ask us how our business is doing, it won't bring us more business to go into a long spiel about our lack of clients during the last week, the difficult client of two weeks ago, and our insecurities. Nor is it their business to know exactly how we're doing. Yet, if we continually say "Everything's wonderful!" we might believe our own pronouncements. How can we handle the pressures of the public and the necessities of our private selves?

In the beginning of my business, I chose one friend who was not in the film industry – my Quaker friend, Cathleen – and told her I wanted one place to go where I could be totally vulnerable and know none of my insecurities, or failures, would be reported to the wider world. I felt I needed to stay honest about the truth, while recognizing the needs of my business.

As time went on, I chose several other friends within the film industry who I trusted, and who would understand and be sensitive to the problems.

Our spiritual communities can also provide ways for us to be honest and to seek advice. Dr. Marty says, "I make a distinction in one of my books between association and community. Your spiritual community is made up of the people to whom you can confide your secrets and they confide them back." These communities can come in the form of spiritual support groups, or individuals within your community.

Quakers have Clearness Committees which are formed when a Quaker has a concern they wish to discuss. The individual Quaker calls together a small group of people from the Meeting, usually three to five people, and asks a question that needs clarity. I had a Clearness Committee before writing my ninth and most controversial book, about Christian values from the viewpoint of the Democratic Party – *Jesus Rode a Donkey*. I knew it had the potential to divide, rather than unite people, which was not something I wanted to do. But it was an assignment from the publisher, and could be my breakthrough into writing theology books after eight screenwriting books. It interested me, but I also realized it could bring great trouble upon me. I asked for advice, and reached clarity to write it, but decided to have several Christian Republican readers who would help me be truthful, kind, and moderate. And the Committee helped me recognize I would get some hate mail (I did) and get raked over the coals by some (I did), but I might also do a service. There was a way to go gently into the fray, and to be prepared for the consequences.

Others form a Spiritual Committee to help them assess decisions, and to share their truth. Karen Ball is the executive editor for fiction for B & H Publishing Group, which is the publishing arm of LifeWay, the largest supplier of Christian materials in the world. In addition, she is a best-selling novelist. She says, "I've formed an advisory board for my career as an editor and writer. This is a group of people who've known me for years, some in the publishing world, some just in life. People who will speak truth to me, even when it's hard. I have many opportunities that come to me, both in my work as an editor and an author, but just because you are able to do something, doesn't mean you should. I've discovered too often, though I pray about decisions, I get distracted from what matters most and say 'yes' when I should say 'no', and vice versa. So I've asked my board to help me assess decisions, to consider them prayerfully and then come together and dialogue. The goal is to move in wisdom rather than emotion, to stay focused on those tasks God wants me doing, not what I think will be fun or expedient or beneficial. Because his perspective is what matters most."

These committees can be helpful for anyone who faces difficult decisions or wants help to stay on track with their work. When there's a tyranny of opinions, a Clearness Committee can help find clarity. If you form a Clearness or Spiritual Committee, look for wise and discerning people who you trust, but who won't so much tell you what to do, as help you in your seeking. Be careful of adding toxic or negative people to the team. Or people who think they know what's best for you. This is to help you find clearness, not to have someone else tell you what to do. They can come from many walks of life, and can come with many different types of knowledge. A meeting of an hour or two does much to lead to clearness about the next steps.

Learning to risk again

It isn't just truth we need to follow. But doing the will of God demands risk and expansion. With success can come comfort. We know who we are and others know who we are. No longer do we have to try, and try again, and even compromise to get a job at all. We become good at what we do and comfortable doing it. We are known for it, admired for it, respected for it, and sometimes envied for it. Life is good, and sweet, and safe.

Although this may work in many jobs, it doesn't work well when we are asked to be creative and to sustain our creativity through many years. Going beyond our safety zone is absolutely essential for those in the arts and for those in the sciences. Making new discoveries is an essential part of the work.

There is a phrase writers and actors often use to encourage themselves to keep risking and to stay creative in their work – "Kill the darlings!" The phrase has been used by William Faulkner, and by Sir Arthur Quiller-Couch in the book *On the Art of Writing* (1916), and by Luc Sante. It's also a phrase used in the Bible, in Hosea 9:16 (in the NKJV and the NJB translations), although it's used there in quite a different way.

The phrase means creative people need to stop doing those things that got them by so easily in the past. Whether it's a little twitch, a certain smile, a certain walk, there's a temptation for an actor to do whatever worked in the last role. Perhaps, for the writer, it's a turn of phrase that got them acclaim, or certain character idiosyncrasies they continually write into all of their characters. The most creative people continue to find original ways of doing their work.

Continuing to risk can be difficult. Making all things new – once again – can be a challenge.

Author T. Davis Bunn, who is American but is currently living part time in England, has written over forty books, many of them best sellers. He discovered the problem of getting too comfortable when, in 1998, six of his books in a row hit the top five. Suddenly Davis found himself deluged with publishing offers. "After years of struggling to get noticed, I was being contacted by people I've never met, representing companies who had never spoken with me before. They were offering what for me were huge deals – three books, five, seven. At this point, my wife Isabella urged me to take a step back, and pray, not over the offers, but rather the direction. This was the time to slow down, she said, and she was right. 'You want to leave a legacy through your writing. You want to have control over what you do. This is the time to set your boundaries on how you're going to do this, and not let your head or other people push you into how this is going to be defined.'"

There were two major upshots of this difficult but important pause. First, Davis added more time to each deadline, so he could take as long as each book required for the edits. This is not to say that stress has been erased. If success breeds anything, it is a constant increase in stress levels. But adding this time meant each book could be honed to the best of his ability, not shot out according to an uncomfortable timeline. Secondly, Davis inserted ten weeks into every year that were not under contract. This allowed him time for experimentation, and for trying out different and risky ideas.

This became extremely important because the contracts he did accept (Davis now writes one book each year for the mainstream, and one for a Christian publisher) included very specific rules and boundaries and limits for these books, including specific characters he had to incorporate.

Davis says: "It's essential as a creative artist to maintain a sense of risk. Pushing beyond the comfort zone is vital. Every artist needs to establish some way to continue the challenge of creative expansion and personal growth."

Keeping our identity, maintaining our integrity

When we become important, others can begin creating their own definitions of who we are. We can be thrown around by others' opinions and expectations of us, and try to fit into the mold they've created. We lose our identities, but also lose our integrity, as we try to be all things to other people. Our friendships and our spiritual and support communities help keep us honest. But stepping out with our integrity still creates risks.

Davis says: "When I re-read my work for one book, I felt it was deeply flawed and it needed a thorough rewrite. I knew it wasn't good enough. Yet, because this was a new publishing relationship, it was risky to tell them I now needed another ten weeks to do my own rewrites. But because there had been this spiritual calm behind this deal, I was able to ask for this with a certain amount of peace. And they agreed, even though it meant the publication date would need to be pushed back – something authors generally shouldn't do with their publishers."

Joseph and his amazing importance

We can learn something about how to handle importance, and how not to handle importance, by looking at the story of Joseph, who was very important, then not important, and then important again.

The story is told in Genesis. Joseph was the best-loved son of his father, Jacob, and the least loved son by most of his brothers, who were jealous of him, and hated all the advantages he seemed to have. With importance, can come resentment and a desire for revenge. And the brothers definitely wanted to get rid of him. Joseph as a boy could be considered arrogant and full of himself. He had a dream about how his brothers would one day bow down to him, which he immediately reported to his brothers. This did little to endear him to them. Finally, the brothers saw a chance to get rid of him. When Joseph brought food to his brothers while they were tending the flock of sheep, they plotted to kill him. Brother Reuben, who was a bit nicer than the other brothers, suggested an alternative – to throw him into a well. Reuben planned to rescue Joseph later. Instead, the brothers decided to sell Joseph into slavery. Joseph was taken to Egypt and the brothers told their father he was killed by a wild animal.

Rather than losing his importance, Joseph became important to Potiphar, an Egyptian official and commander of the guard. He was made an important part of the household, entrusted with Potiphar's possessions, and put in charge of the household.

But Potiphar's wife wanted to seduce him, perhaps because he was handsome, perhaps also because he was important. Joseph continually said "no" until she tricked him and lied, saying he had slept with her. Joseph was thrown into jail.

Although Joseph was no longer important to Potiphar, he became important to the jailer, who put him in charge of all the prisoners. And the Bible repeats again, "Yahweh made everything he undertook successful."[79]

Shortly afterwards, two of the King's court were put into jail, and both had dreams. When Joseph saw them the next morning, looking gloomy, he was sensitive to them and asked about the problem. They said no one could interpret their dreams. But Joseph could. He interpreted the dreams, which helped one official to regain his position. Joseph asked him to remember him, but the official didn't. So Joseph remained another two years in jail.

But two years later, Pharaoh had a dream and could find no one to interpret it. Finally Joseph was summoned and he interpreted it. Pharaoh realized here was a man who was intelligent and wise. Joseph was then made Governor of all of Egypt.

During the time of famine which Joseph had predicted, his family was suffering back home. When they heard Egypt had food, Jacob sent his sons there to get food. Eventually, Joseph was reunited with his brothers. He forgave them, and saw all these trials as part of God's will.

Joseph seems to have made many good decisions about his importance, once he was taken down to size and got over his youthful arrogance. He waited. He responded when someone had a need. He made friends with those around him, no matter what their status was. He kept his integrity in spite of temptations and forces that threatened to take it away. He was generous. He forgave those who had hurt him. Perhaps, most important, he saw the hand of God in the many twists and turns of his life.

Questions for discussion

1. Do you have certain fears about being famous and being important? What are your greatest concerns?
2. If you met these problems that come with fame, how would you handle them?
3. Watch some films that show a more private person becoming more important. Some possibilities are *Norma Rae, Wall Street, Erin Brockovich, The Lord of the Rings, Quiz Show, Working Girl, The Devil's Advocate*. Did they handle their new-found importance well, or not?
4. Dr. Marty said Nebraska and Chicago are his reference points which keep him grounded. What are your reference points?
5. Who helps you overcome your barriers to success?

Scripture to consider

Read some of the Scripture about being humbled and being exalted: 1 Chronicles 25:5; 29:12; Joshua 4:14; Psalms 37:34; 46:10; Matthew 23:12; Luke 14:11; 18:14.

Part 2

Traveling the Rocky Road

CHAPTER 5

Meeting the Seven Deadly Sins

Adam ate the apple, and our teeth still ache.

Hungarian proverb

Along the road to success, you'll meet the Seven Deadly Sins of envy (sometimes called jealousy), covetousness (sometimes called greed or avarice), lust, anger (sometimes called wrath), pride, gluttony and sloth. Some of them will command your attention more than others. Some will grab you, clutch you, tempt you, and seduce you. Others will demand just a passing glance with, perhaps, a brief relationship. I'm not convinced anyone moving toward professional success will ever totally escape them.

Since success is usually defined in the world's terms – fame, money, prestige, opportunity, power and increased respect and admiration – it is almost a given that these sins will be on the success path. They live there, and find their victims particularly vulnerable. To clutch someone who has clout and influence is a far greater victory for the Deadly Sins than their many smaller victories with those who might experience greed, but will never get what they desire. The Deadly Sins want to have influence in the world, and although they'll be happy to play with anyone, they particularly love those with power.

Many don't like to use the word "sin", since it seems so medieval and seems to be of little use in our lives, where we believe there are simply problems and flaws and a few mistakes along the way. But it's imperative we realize that the repercussions of sin are tragic, real, and are responsible for all the evil in the world.

If we don't recognize these sins, their clutches can, indeed, be terrible. We downplay them, which gives them total power over our lives and destroys any possibility of us truly doing good in the world.

As Cain was told in Genesis, "Sin is crouching at your door, but you may conquer it."[80] And if we choose, we can.

Although there is probably no one particular order in which we'll all meet them, often on the road to success they begin with the green-eyed giant of envy.

Envy wreaketh from our every pore

Envy can be a great motivator. At the beginning, it looks as if it's simply telling us what we want. We see something – another person's success and opportunity, their home which is larger than our one-room apartment, their car which actually runs and rarely needs to be fixed, their spouse who is well respected as opposed to our lack of dates, the admiration they receive for their work, as opposed to no one noticing our own – and we want it, badly.

I have heard more than one person say envy can be good, because it helps us recognize what we want. This is one way to turn this twinge of envy into something positive. Overcoming the feeling of envy by recognizing our desires can help us understand our true identity and what we want in our lives, and what we don't want – provided, of course, that what we want is in tune with what the Holy Spirit wants.

But I'm not sure these people are really talking about the sin of envy, but about the twinge of desire. The sin of envy is far more powerful and tragic. It begins with a pit in the stomach. It can twist and turn us, eating away at us and creating a hunger that creates a feeling of lack within us, and believes there is affluence for everyone else whom we consider above us. It is insatiable, and wants everything for us, and wants to deprive others.

Envy blindsides us. It keeps our focus only on the affluent whom we see as ultimately important. It sees life in purely materialistic terms. It cares about how the world looks at us, and believes *things* are what gives us our self-worth. These things become the only vista in our worldview. Gone is any admiration or respect for the poor woman creating community spirit in her neighborhood. Or for the struggling worker, eking out a living from a small business and creating a loving home. Or for the kindness of the man in the wheelchair down the street, who talks and listens to our children every day on their way home from school.

Envy decides who, and what, is important and there is no discussion about it. Envy can only see things, and the immediate effect of things, whether it's the respect of the applauding crowds, or the newspaper articles about the rich man, or the blogs and Google hits that prove our importance, or the many accoutrements that come from wealth.

Envy makes us forget who we truly are and what we truly want.

Some years ago, I took a seminar where we were

asked to do affirmations about what we wanted and to create collages which visualized those things we desired in our lives. The exercise, in itself, can be helpful, since it can help us see the possibility that we can be prosperous. We begin to see the possibility of having more success on many different levels, including the material level.

But when I think of my collage, I remember the pictures, torn from magazines, of fancy, modern, large homes, a red Porsche, a very handsome and obviously rich man who I could visualize as my husband, fawning over me. Most of my pictures had no real connection with me and what I truly wanted, only what I thought I wanted.

As I continued to visualize and affirm what I thought I wanted, I began to lose sight of my true goals. I was entering into the film industry and thought I wanted to be a vice-president of a studio, dining at the finest restaurants and hob-nobbing with the rich and famous. I imagined my name in the paper – starting, of course, with my small-town paper in Peshtigo, Wisconsin, which I was sure would be tremendously interested in a "small town girl makes good" story. Then, of course, I'd be written up in the trade papers, perhaps the *L.A. Times*.

I began to think more about the accolades around me than my larger goal of helping others make better films. I watched the glitzy people, and forgot there was nothing very glitzy about me, nor would there ever be. It simply was not who I was.

Over the years, as I began to rethink that collage, I realized there's nothing wrong with thinking about, visualizing, cutting out pictures of what we really want. But that collage was not a true representation of my real goals. It was about the kind of goals I thought I was supposed to have.

When envy begins to grab us, we need to keep going back to our original, true goals. Envy cares more about what other people think, than about what we think. If we can remember what is truly important to us, we can affirm that and keep an eye on the goal, whether or not it's affirmed by others. We have to keep remembering who we are, and what's important to us, not what we think is supposed to be important. By doing this, we can find a more authentic identity.

We can also be blindsided by envy, since sometimes it's not our envy that's the problem, but other people's envy of us. In fact, our fear of their envy can be so great, it can affect our ability to be successful.

Many times people are envious of us because we do little to encourage them on their own path to success. We can learn to counter envy through another spiritual discipline: learning to support others. We can make sure we don't give someone a reason to envy us. If we're supportive and encouraging, celebrate the victories of others, look for opportunities to nurture the success of others, and wish others well, we learn to connect with others, rather than separate from them. Everyone needs support and affirmation, but envy can separate us from those we consider above us. Support and encouragement overcome the pinch of envy.

We can also overcome envy by seeing success as about opportunity, not as about things. And when envy dangles her glitzy things in front of our eyes, we can look more closely and more authentically, to see if this is something we truly desire, that truly serves us, or if we're buying into the world's desires, even though it has nothing to do with us.

Envy can be a tempting trickster, since sometimes it's difficult to know whether what is dangled in front of us is a temptation, or a blessing. Is this envy showing us something she thinks we should want, or is this God presenting a blessing?

True identity leads you to what your heart desires, not what others think you should desire. True identity is worth listening to. When you get there, rather than leaving you empty and desiring more, it nurtures your success.

Thou shalt not covet

Covetousness, sometimes called greed, is a close sister to envy. In many descriptions of the Seven Deadly Sins, greed or avarice is sometimes another name for covetousness and sometimes it's equated with envy. Whereas envy can look upon what it desires from afar, covetousness comes closer. It's next door. In Exodus, in the Hebrew Scriptures, the Ten Commandments say, "You shall not covet your neighbor's house; you shall not covet your neighbor's wife, or his male servant, nor his female servant, nor his ox, nor his donkey, or anything that is your neighbor's."[81] This becomes very specific.

The covetousness that comes from wanting something from someone close to us – whether family or neighbor or friend or colleague – guarantees we cannot have an equal and supportive relationship with our neighbor. It leads to deceit and betrayal. On the one hand, we seek to establish good relationships with those closest to us. On the other hand, we are secretly desiring what they have, and wishing they didn't have it and we had it instead. As one character says in the film *When Harry Met Sally*, "I want what she's having."

To get what we covet usually demands manipulation. Ego often comes to the forefront. Whereas envy often believes she's not deserving of the desire and couldn't possibly have it, covetousness believes if it can be next door, it can also be in our own backyard. If the neighbor has it, there's no reason for us not to also have it. Whereas envy creates a pit in our stomach that desires to be filled, but doesn't know how to fill it, covetousness feels it's all within our grasp. It's just a sideyard away.

When we covet, we have to be two-faced. Our desire to have good relationships with those closest to us leads to words of support for others. Our desire to have what they're having, leads to our words belying our actions.

Covetousness can be like a cancer of the eyes. Whereas envy resides in the gut, covetousness is in the eyes – noticing, watching, waiting, peering. And it's like a hole in the heart where the normal heart connections are no longer there. Our natural desires to connect with the neighbor are cut off. We forget what's really important – working together in community is how we all get what we want. We forget our neighbor is often willing to help us – often by being willing to share their metaphoric oxen or servant. Instead we substitute competition for neighborliness.

There seem to be two emotions when we covet. On the one hand, we might feel hurt someone who seems so like us has what we want and what we don't seem to be able to get. On the other hand, we might feel almost sick about their success, even though we have to hide these feelings.

Whereas envy would like to grab, but usually can't because it's too far away, covetousness knows grabbing cannot be done directly. The action of covetousness is more like a weasel, analyzing the opportunities, looking for the way in, strategizing the moment when the desire can lead to action.

Covetousness separates. When one covets another, it is impossible for those two people to relate as equals, or as supporters. It is impossible to have friendly relationships with someone who covets us, or who has the things we covet.

How to break the cycle of coveting? Sometimes we can break the cycle by sharing with those who covet what we have. We can lend them our metaphoric oxen or help them out with the metaphoric tools of our trade (although hopefully we will not lend them our spouse!). We can let them know about the struggles we've gone through to achieve success. We can let them know their struggles are also struggles we've experienced and offer our support, insight, or compassion. We can help them on their journey to success, sharing the secrets we've learned to make the journey shorter. We can let them know about the hard work we've gone through, knowing many want everything now – and don't understand the process. True covetousness doesn't want to go through the process. It simply wants to steal the results.

The lust for life and everything else

We often think of lust as sexual desire, sometimes leading to uncontrollable sex with one person, sometimes the constant desire and need of many partners. Although lust or lechery is usually equated with the excessive desire for sex, it is sometimes considered to be any excessive

141

desire. It is sometimes humorously asked, "How much sex (or anything else) is enough?" The answer may be, "When sex becomes more important than the loved one you're having it with."

Some years ago, my husband, who is both a massage therapist and an acupuncturist, told me he had a massage client who came in for his weekly massage, totally depleted. He had been having an orgy for a week. Peter said he had never seen anyone so totally exhausted – to the point where Peter thought he might become permanently ill, or even die. Peter explained that this kind of lust damages the whole body as well as the mind and soul. Too much is not a good thing.

Lust is a distortion of a relationship. Rather than focusing on the other person, and being a giver, lust is a taker. It wants parts of the person, not the whole person. It wants to *get* pleasure, rather than to *give* mutual pleasure. It is more interested in seduction than honesty, more interested in strategy than in sharing.

In our professional lives, lust can work on many different levels, all of them harmful to at least one of the partners. In an unequal relationship, lust becomes the bargaining tool. Sometimes the bargain comes from the more powerful, as the boss wants to take more and more from the less powerful, often insisting on a sexual response in order for the other person to keep the job. Sometimes it's the bargaining tool by the powerless who are willing to sell themselves, in one way or another, to get the job, the money, or the material possessions.

Whereas love-making respects boundaries, lust crosses boundaries. Whereas love-making is a part of life, lust becomes the whole of one's vision. In our professional lives, this deadly sin becomes disruptive of our goals. It's difficult to focus on the job when the heaving breasts or the tight T-shirt are taking all of our attention.

Like envy, lust confuses us. We think we want something, but it's not at all what we want. It keeps us from our goal of a well-rounded life where our love life and our professional life can integrate with balance.

Many women lust after a Clint Eastwood type, even though they have nothing in common with a High Plains Drifter or the silent gunfighter type. Many men lust after the modern Marilyn Monroe, in any of the various forms, even though they would have nothing in common with her. Many fall in love with a certain "look", although there is no possibility of a loving relationship between them and the tall, dark, handsome manipulator or the beautiful, voluptuous woman who has seduced them with good looks and sweet words, but with nothing else.

Lust consumes us, rather than frees us. It narrows our vistas, rather than expands them. And it diminishes the human being to the person's parts rather than to their full complexity.

Naturally, all of us have probably experienced lust in our hearts and our loins, and the desire and attraction for another person is a normal reaction. The spiritual discipline which can often help overcome lust comes from changing lust to appreciation. My Jungian therapist (the excellent cheap one mentioned in Chapter 3!) pointed out to me that those things we want can help us recognize what we appreciate if we don't give them power over us. When we find ourselves attracted to someone who is clearly inappropriate (perhaps because we're married, perhaps because the person truly isn't our type), we might ask ourselves: "What do I appreciate about this person?" We can then see that part of this attraction is a good thing. Usually the person is attractive, but there's more to it than that. The person might also be fun, kind, smart, generous, and/or caring – all qualities that are worthy of being appreciated. If we tell ourselves, "This is normal, there are good qualities here", lust usually doesn't want to stick around, since it has lost its power over us.

Usually we meet greed, covetousness and lust when we're climbing the ladder and trying to get to the top. Rather than freeing us, they confuse us. We lose our identities, and often lose our focus because we don't know for sure what we want and why we want it. They put everything in the world's terms, and make promises that when we get what we desire, all will be well. So we continue to climb the wrong ladder. We get lost on the wrong path. We become obsessed with something that won't give us any satisfaction, even if we can get it.

And when we arrive at the goal, we encounter other sins that bring us into new forms of bondage.

The pervasive hunger of gluttony

Gluttony is deceptive, because it believes we truly need everything and it sets up its world so we think what we desire is what we truly need. Gluttony wants to gulp down, to over-indulge and over-consume. Gluttony believes if you don't have the right car, you don't get hired, so you suddenly need the expensive car. If you don't have the trophy wife or trophy husband, you won't be able to get invited to the right parties where all the schmoozing goes on, so you hunger for the right spouse who can serve you, in order that you can become more successful. The all-consuming desire becomes an absolute need and it will never occur to you, maybe it's not necessary.

Gluttony desires excess. Gluttony believes in entitlement. It needs to constantly feed itself, bringing everything into itself.

Although gluttony is sometimes thought of as simply overeating, it goes beyond a matter of food. It's the desire for more and more and more, whether we truly want it or not. Anything that is out there, we want for ourselves. There is to be no sharing. There is to be no differentiation between one thing and another. It is the desire for getting and getting and getting. It is the consumerism that expresses itself in many ways. Although, at first, we do it to get filled up, ultimately it depletes our energy, our resources, and never satisfies.

When I lived in Hollywood, I met a famous actress who was down on her luck. She had been one of the best-known soap opera actresses for a period of time, and now seemed to have virtually nothing. I asked her what happened. She explained, "I had plenty of money, so when I went shopping and saw something I liked, I bought it in every color. I could never wear them all and quickly got tired of them and then went out and did the same with something else."

Around this same time, I met an executive in the film industry who clearly was making plenty of money. She told me she went to a very large flea-market every Saturday. I asked if she just wandered around for fun or bought something. She replied, "Oh, I buy a number of things every week." I asked where she put it all, figuring that doing that for a month or two would fill up a house rather quickly. She replied, "I put it in the house for a while, but my house is now so filled, so a lot of it is just stored in the basement."

When success first comes along, and we suddenly have more money than we know what to do with, it may be natural to go through a (hopefully short) spending spree. But there is something else going on here that shows a loss of control and a value system based on materialistic things surrounding us. The flea-market woman lost her job shortly after that. The actress wanted to go back to college, and although she did go back, she struggled for years because she never had a sense of balance when she had been blessed with prosperity.

There are innumerable stories of people who suffer from gluttony and have depleted all their resources. The stars who once had millions of dollars, and now have none. The alcoholics drinking up the little money their family has. The stock-brokers who gamble everyone else's money, and their own, and fill themselves and their houses and garages with status symbols.

Gluttony never shares. It has no concern for anyone outside its own circle – anyone who cannot immediately serve its desires. It's active. It takes. It consumes. It gobbles up. It goes after what it wants, with no regard for anyone's feelings or needs.

Gluttony has a tricky boundary. It's not the enjoyment of a lovely meal with dessert and all the trimmings. It has nothing to do with the fulfillment of our needs, but it has everything to do with excess.

In our professional lives, the superficial activity we do to fill ourselves can leave us feeling empty. Our belief that we need more and more of anything leads to frenetic activity that believes that addition is more important than subtraction, that bigger is better than less.

Gluttony is not just an individual problem, but a social problem, since many First World societies use up far more than their share of resources. It is a natural part of our psyche to think we deserve whatever we can grab. Gluttony withholds from the needy in order to absorb everything for itself.

Since gluttony reaches out to bring everything into itself, we might wonder how one overcomes this all-consuming desire. Perhaps it is best done by the spiritual practice of detachment.

Many religions ask us to be truly involved in our world. Jesus never turned his back on the things of the world – the sicknesses, those who were rejected, even those who had plenty of money and power. Instead, he was involved in the world, without being in the clutches of the world's values.

Non-attachment means we can enjoy many things in the world. We can enjoy our home, our car, perhaps jewelry we love, a special piece of art, some favorite piece of clothing. But if it were taken away from us, we would not mourn its loss (well, not for very long, at least!), since we know these things are not ultimate. We would keep our spiritual center and know the ultimate relationship is not with things, but with God. We enjoy the material things, but are not attached to them.

When we overcome our attachment, and our gluttonous desires, we realize we don't need all of these things. We might still have hopes and expectations, but we don't fall apart if we don't get them. They are just things.

There are exercises to do that can help us detach from gluttony when we feel too involved with the things of the world. Years ago, when I was doing the Ignatian

Exercises (which were designed by St. Ignatius during the Middle Ages to develop our spiritual lives), my spiritual director suggested I take down all the pictures and objects in my apartment that gave me great pleasure and create rooms which were bare. He wanted to teach me these were not of any ultimate importance, and I could be happy and live easily without them. I took them down for about two weeks and found all was just fine. I didn't need them. When I reached the point of freedom from the objects, he recommended I put them back and enjoy them. It was an excellent way to understand how little we need and how simple our lives can be.

This non-attachment works against the frenetic activity and overwhelming materialism of gluttony. By detaching ourselves from these things, by meditating about what is necessary and what is not, we can better go with the flow of life, and allow what is needed to come to us naturally, without anxiety, without grabbing and without excessive activity on our part.

The white heat of anger and rage

What's wrong with anger? Many of us have spent some time in therapy, getting in touch with our emotions, expressing rather than hiding our anger. We know Jesus got so furious at the money-changers in front of the temple that he overturned their tables, yelled and screamed at them, and made a whip and went after them. It doesn't sound like "gentle Jesus, meek and mild." We all can be confused when anger is mentioned as one of the Seven Deadly Sins, and then we're told this story of his tremendous anger. What is going on here? When is anger righteous anger? When does anger become deadly?

Righteous anger calls a spade a spade. It discerns injustice, oppression, divisions, and it discerns the presence of the Seven Deadly Sins. It recognizes the destructiveness of evil and knows the natural and normal response should be to call attention to – sometimes with a certain amount of passion, heat, and fury – what is terribly wrong. Righteous anger hopes to remedy while giving an opportunity for a change of heart. In the best of all possible worlds, our righteous anger should leave us, and others, open to the possibility of solutions.

The deadly sin of anger is divisive. It pushes away. It's usually filled with pride, and is less concerned with what is right than with guarding its position. It is a "How dare you!" response!

Anger can be like a white heat, whether we give it, or whether we are on the receiving end. It can be one of the most deadly of the sins, leading to revenge, assault, and murder.

Many of us have two different responses to anger. For some, anger immobilizes us. If you grew up in a fairly calm household, you may have not had much experience with anger and you may not have the skills to handle it. If you grew up in an emotionally passionate and expressive household, you may deal with anger by giving back what you've just received.

Both of these responses seem counterproductive. Yet, in our work life, we do encounter the anger of others. There's no reason for us to deal with it by pretending we're a ninety-pound weakling or a two-ton gorilla. There has to be a better way.

I asked a friend of mine, who's a psychologist, how

she deals with the anger of another while still preserving her own integrity. She told me: "I make it clear I have boundaries and let the person know not to yell at me, and not to talk to me that way. I then tell the person, 'If you have something to say to me, I can hear it better if you talk more softly. If we have something to resolve together, then let's do it together. I can't hear what you're saying with all the fire around it.'" She says usually this keeps the other person from throwing fire at her.

Personal relationships and professional relationships can create different sets of problems. The niceties and respect that exist between friends and spouses can be missing when we have to overcome deadly anger in our professions. Although we may desire to deal with anger spiritually, this can be difficult, because the heat of our own anger or the anger of another takes away any desire to turn this problem over to God. Sometimes we can't see our way through to calling on the Spirit to help, because we're too hurt and too caught up in the hell of judgment. This might be judgment about how wrong the angry person is or it might be the judgment of how right we are to be angry at that person. Either way, self-righteousness has blocked our openness to talking to God about it.

Sometimes, the best way to deal with anger is to simply retreat for a while, perhaps go to a quiet place and just sit in silence, pray or meditate, and try to quiet the turmoil so some discernment can get through to us. If possible, it's good to follow the biblical suggestion: "Don't let the sun go down on your anger." Anger in one person creates turmoil in another. It is so pervasive, it can color our decisions and our everyday peace of mind. It fills us with negative thoughts and with strategies of how to prove ourselves right and to prove them wrong, or how to get back at them for being so mean to us.

Although many of the Seven Deadly Sins are handled over a long period of time as we struggle with our lust or greed or envy, anger is relational and needs to be handled quickly. Unresolved anger eats away at us. It stops our productivity, and often leads to sickness and death.

Uncaring sloth

Sloth doesn't care. It's not just about an occasional laziness. Sloth isn't the relaxation we all need when we slow down, hang out, kick back, and do nothing. There's nothing really dangerous about that and in most cases, this slowing down is necessary for a balanced professional life. Don't mistake sloth for relaxation.

One of my friends once explained to me how she sees sloth operating in the corporate world. She said some of her colleagues learned to do just enough to get by without getting fired. They figured out the lowest common denominator and made sure nothing they did rocked the boat, called attention to itself, did anything that could be considered provocative.

In its gentler side (and sloth may be one of the few sins that has a less dangerous side), it refuses to cooperate, or to collaborate, or to contribute. It sits back and lets everyone else do all the work.

On the surface, this might seem useless, but not necessarily dangerous. But all the Seven Deadly Sins are deadly. What does sloth do, since it doesn't seem to do much?

Sloth tempts us to give up. It pulls us back and tells us what we do doesn't matter, it's not worth doing, no one is going to care anyway, it's far too difficult to try, so don't bother. It convinces us our contributions are unnecessary and unimportant.

The world around us colludes with sloth. No matter what our profession, we continually come across those who don't care and we buy into their judgment. We give our power over to the opinions of others and put down the pen and throw in the towel. Nothing seems worth it.

In doing so, the important work we want to do in the world never happens. Evil prevails and good dies out. Much of the goodness in the world halts, not because of the active evil that is being done, but the passive evil that occurs because of those who do nothing. What seems on the surface to be a quiet little passive sin is one of the reasons why so much evil survives.

Sloth collaborates with the other sins by allowing them to have power over us so we give up. It allows the pride of others to take over. It lets lust have its way, because it believes that it doesn't matter who you sleep with and it's easier not to say anything than to say "no". And the righteous anger of others has no effect on sloth.

Sloth tempts us to stop. When we work with slothful people, it becomes particularly difficult in our professional lives. No matter what our profession, most of the work we do is collaborative. This is particularly true in the film industry and the publishing industry – the two worlds which I know the best. Sometimes others consider the work of the screenwriter to be a solitary job, but the screenwriter's work is dependent upon the director, actors, and producers to make the film and the distributors to get it out in the theaters. A fiction or non-fiction writer has to work with a publisher, an editor, a publicist, public relations people and distributors, so that all the work that goes into writing a book has a chance to be seen. Sloth makes promises. It just doesn't keep them. We expect other members of our team to do their work. Sloth never does its part, which can destroy a project that may have taken years to come to fruition.

Sloth is dishonest. It's not a straight shooter. It usually won't tell you what it means. There are many passive-aggressive people who have made good friends with sloth. They tell you they'll do something, but they don't. They promise they'll meet deadlines, but they don't. They miss deadlines, take a vacation or take days off without telling others they won't be around, and then make a whole new set of promises which are never kept.

Whereas most of the Seven Deadly Sins are hurtful, the sloth of others can simply drive us crazy over its passivity. It diminishes our work. It can also bring our work to a halt, since much of what we do in any job is dependent upon others. It is a saboteur, because it has no responsiveness or sensitivity to the hard work of others. It can immobilize us and bring us to a halt, suggesting our work is meaningless and worthless and not worth all that energy.

Because sloth is sly, we're often not warned we're getting into a relationship with it. We might think we're working with a relaxed and easy-going guy we expect to do his share and be fun. Everything on the surface might look just fine. Instead, we find all of our efforts have been erased, by sloth doing nothing.

If we believe the world moves forward by good works, then it's clear the sabotage of sloth forces us to go backward, rather than forward. We can see it socially. The electrical grids that were supposed to be taken care of, weren't. And a blackout affected millions. The road that was supposed to be fixed, wasn't, and people were killed. The information that was supposed to be shared before the attacks of 9/11 wasn't, and the repercussions were enormous. Sloth ignores warnings. It sits back. It doesn't take anything seriously, and serious and tragic happenings occur as a result.

Spiritually, when sloth asks us to give up, it can be helpful to slow down, relax, take a deep breath. Sometimes, we can handle sloth in our own lives by giving in to passivity for a few days. If we feel re-energized at the end of a few days, we know it's not been sloth, it's been the need to regroup. If the feeling continues, then we may have to put aside time to move forward by turning to our creative side to recreate, and not to allow sloth to halt and destroy.

Pride and the fall

Whereas envy resides in the pit of the stomach, pride is in our head. We feel full of ourselves. Pride puffs itself up, becoming invulnerable so no one can prick our lofty self. Pride not only believes we are the best, but no one can touch us. Nothing can get through to pride. It receives nothing from anyone else, considers nothing from anyone else, collaborates with no one outside itself. It refuses to let anyone in, since pride believes it has no need for anyone else.

Although we may meet pride at the beginning of our career, which may sometimes masquerade as braggadocio because of our insecurity, most of the time pride envelops us when we start to do well. When we're at the top of our game. When we've become rich and famous and consider ourselves the best there is.

This position is difficult to hang on to. Since someone will always come along to challenge this, pride makes sure nothing gets through. For many successful people, pride surrounds itself with the keepers of the gates. It makes sure anyone who tells us anything different than praise won't be allowed through. It is in desperate need to continue to uphold its own image, so only those who mirror pride's self-image are allowed in. Their job is to reflect and magnify pride's beauty and rightness, and to make sure that no other possible interpretation can get through.

Pride keeps us from growing. Since we are not open to any other possibilities, we can only continue to uphold the image of ourselves we set in stone when we received that first glorious praise, or when the first newspaper article was published about us, or when we were first hired for a job and told we were the best and the brightest. Pride believes there is nothing more to learn and there is no one worthy of contributing anything to us.

It is no wonder pride goes before the fall. In any profession, we are asked to continue to grow, change, transform, be innovative, try new things, and keep up with the evolution of our profession. Pride is stuck, absolutely stuck, and cannot change, even though everything around it might be changing.

In order to uphold its lofty self, pride relies heavily on the ego. It has to diminish others in order to remain on its high perch looking down. And, of course, from this lofty perch, everyone does look small and insignificant.

Pride is both clever and stupid. It knows how to convince others about its own importance. But because it refuses to take everything into consideration when making a decision, or doing a job, its lack of wisdom causes tragic errors.

In 1988, I was invited to New Zealand by the New Zealand Film Commission to train a group of professionals as script consultants. My prideful self wondered if I really wanted to raise up competition to my work, since some of my consulting work came from New Zealand. I struggled with pride for a few weeks and realized there was only one way for me to overcome my thinking. I had to find a way to overcome these feelings of competition, loneliness, and isolation. I began to think of my work as part of a larger goal than myself. Realizing pride puts itself up as the only one who can do everything necessary, I tried to think of my job as part of a much larger picture. I realized I, by myself, couldn't make better films. But together with many others working toward the same goal, we might have a chance. I began to redefine my goal. Rather than choosing a goal such as "Getting more clients" or "Making more money through my work", I thought of my goal as "Helping others make better films." I began to see myself as part of a new movement of independent script consultants working with many writers and producers and companies to try to accomplish that objective. I began to support those who I saw also working for these high ideals.

Once I made the decision to share my knowledge with others, I set off to teach my first Master Class in Script Consulting in New Zealand. The New Zealand Film Commission sent me a Business Class ticket and I decided that was the proof of how very important I was. (There goes pride again!) As I got on the plane, I said some stupid words that could only come from invulnerable pride. My husband wished me a safe voyage and I replied, "Don't worry, honey, nobody ever dies in Business Class" as I took my seat in 7B. I learned quickly the level of my stupidity. Six weeks later, on that same United Airline flight to New Zealand, a hole was blown in the side of the plane, sucking out several passengers, including the one who sat in 7B. It became clear to me I wasn't invulnerable and it was time to get off my high horse.

As we progress in our careers, pride can take us to a lonely place. Pride has no interest in serving. It is not collaborative and eventually falls because there are no relationships to uphold it. We have to preserve our position as the King or Queen of the Mountain and can't admit there are many other very talented people doing work similar to us. Pride can keep us from being able to trade ideas with others, to discuss problems in our work, to support others and be supported, and to allow our work to evolve. Eventually, we fall.

When I wrote *When Women Call the Shots*, I interviewed the actress, Jane Wyman, who explained the problem about pride. She said no matter how far up the person is, if they got there through pride and ego, when they fall, the fall is so long and so hard because there is no one to support them and uphold them on the way down. When the fall comes, it is complete. Sometimes people even celebrate the person's defeat, since they no longer have to deal with the tyrant again.

Of course, those who are prideful may have a good run of success for some years. Sometimes people work with those who are prideful, because power often comes with pride and people are forced to work with the egocentric boss. But once they fall, no one is there to help pick up the pieces because no one wants to play with them any more. If no one has to work with them, they don't.

Pride robs us of all the possibilities of growth. It's frozen. It's self-righteous. It is non-transformative. It creates dictators in our world and tyrants in the office. And it keeps us, and our work, from evolving.

Pride may be one of the most prominent sins for many successful people, since the very nature of success brings self-confidence, a sense of achievement, respect and even adulation. Missionary Lisa Borden says this can be very true in her own profession: "Pride would be the sin I have to face in myself. My line of work leads the people back home to give us too much credit for our choice of vocation. We often hear things like, 'You guys are *so* amazing!', 'I could *never* do what you do' and 'You must be a really *special* kind of person.' Pride would like to slip in behind these comments and take up residence in my heart. I can feel myself being tempted to believe I really am something else. In reality, I believe all callings carry a set of sacrifices and benefits with them. While there have been certain times when I had to make the choice to continue on this path that I've been nudged toward, there are plenty of other times when I revel in the freedom I've had to follow my heart. We chose this vocation and it suits us. We are released into it by the support of donors and we recognize that as a gift, not a situation to suffer through. When we are being true to our gifting and heart's desire, there isn't really an acceptable reason for pride, in the negative sense of the word. Thankfulness would be more in order."

How do we defuse the sin of pride? Although we're often told humility is the opposite of pride, and certainly being humble is a good spiritual trait to learn, the way to overcome pride might include some other steps. We might start by affirming our colleagues, identifying special talents, recommending them for jobs we're not able to take or not suited for. We can begin to see our colleagues as team players and begin to mutually help each other. We can join organizations and contribute what we've learned, as well as recognize and support others. We can come off our lofty perch of pride and begin to relate to others. We can learn to contribute to others and instead of asking what we can get from the others, we can ask what we can give.

We can become team players, since pride is isolating, and teamwork leads to collaboration. The people most of us love to work with are the team players. Everyone wants to work with them, and their lives expand rather than contract.

One of my favorite people in the film industry is Ron Howard. I've interviewed him for two of my books, and although I by no means know him well, he is a collaborator who is both generous and humble. His co-workers seem to love working with him because he listens to them, asks their advice, and works *with* them rather than against them. As Ron said to me in one interview, "I hire some of the best people in the world to work with me. Why wouldn't I take advantage of their skills and wisdom and knowledge?"

We can overcome pride through our vulnerability, through our gratitude – recognizing our need for others and for God, sharing our struggles, asking others for advice. Any action we take that connects us with each other forces pride to step aside.

The seven deadly sins are there to stop, not encourage

You may have noticed every one of these sins, in one way or another, stops us from actualizing our talents, from doing good work, from contributing, from evolving in our professional lives. Are they deadly? I think so. We don't need more violence, self-righteousness, divisions, separations, put-downs, and immobilization in our lives. Our goal is to move toward something better, bigger, more inclusive, which pulls us together to create a better world.

Questions for discussion

1. Which of these deadly sins has had the most influence over you? Which one has had the least?
2. Have you been able to overcome these sins through specific spiritual practices? What are they?
3. Can you think of some famous people or people you have known in your own profession who have fallen? Which of the Seven Deadly Sins brought them down?
4. How do each of these sins get in the way of us following our calling?
5. Do you find these sins get in your way at certain times in your journey, but perhaps not at other times? What steps are most apt to bring each of them in front of you?

Scripture to consider

Read some of the passages about sin and evil in the Bible: Genesis 8:21; Deuteronomy 27:9–10; Joshua 22:5; Proverbs 6:16–19; Jeremiah 17:9; Matthew 7:11; Mark 7:15–23; Romans 6:23; 7:18–21; Galatians 5:19–21.

Read about some of the figures in the Bible who have encountered these sins and have felt their power:

Envy: Look at how envy and anger destroyed Saul (1 Samuel 18).

Covetousness: Read about how Abraham thought others would covet his wife and used deceit (Genesis 20).

Lust: Read about Samson and Delilah and David and Bathsheba (Judges 16; 2 Samuel 11–12; 1 Kings 1–2).

Gluttony: Read about how some saw Jesus as a glutton in Matthew 11 and Luke 7. Why would they think that way? Read about the problems of gluttony: Proverbs 23; 28; Titus 1.

Anger: Genesis 49:7; Exodus 11:8; 32; 1 Samuel 20:30; Romans 2:8; Proverbs 22:24.

Sloth: Read how sloth kept others from taking Noah seriously in Genesis 7.

Pride: Read about the pride of those who argued about who is the greatest and who shall sit at the right or left hand of God (Matthew 20:20–27; Mark 10:35–45).

Do other passages come to mind? How is Proverbs 6:16–19 related to these Seven Deadly Sins?

CHAPTER 6

Connecting, not Competing, for Success

Into the community you were called – the call was not meant for you alone; in the community of the called you bear our cross, you struggle, you pray… If you scorn the fellowship of the brethren, you reject the call of Jesus Christ.

Dietrich Bonhoeffer, *Life Together*

When we were young, and just starting to figure out how the world worked, many of us received two different messages about how to get ahead in life. We were told to play well with others, to be kind to the neighboring kids, to get along with everyone (provided they were relatively nice – we weren't expected to get along with the bullies!), and we weren't supposed to judge others by the color of their skin or by whether they were rich or poor. We were taught that all were created equal, and we chose our friends not according to their intelligence, their money, or the lineage of their parents, but by how much fun we could have with them.

We were also taught another way of looking at life. There were people who were considered above us. They were richer, had better jobs, bigger houses, and nicer cars. We were told we must get ahead and were graded according to whether we did better than the others, or worse. Some were judged as having more potential than others, and teachers paid more attention to the better students and less attention to the slow-learners and late-bloomers.

When we entered the world of business, careers, and jobs, these two ways of thinking often fought for our allegiance, but generally the second one won. Competition was the name of the game in almost every kind of business. We were ranked on a line and a hierarchy. We were pitted against each other for jobs and soon learned our place on the corporate ladder or in the pecking order of our business. Whether it was a desire to be the CEO, to win the gold medal, or to have the most successful business, we seemed to exist in a world that ranked everyone by their rungs on an imaginary ladder. We had to learn to be tough to enter this world, and tougher still to maintain our position or to get ahead.

We learned to think competitively, rather than collaboratively. We were ranked on a line that determined who was up and who was down. It didn't take long for us to recognize that the person on top made the rules and enforced them and got all the perks, and everyone else played by the rules the best they could, and tried to move up.

Questioning linear thinking

There are some good things to this linear model. A line or a ladder is one way to measure progress. A line can show direction. It sets the goal. It recognizes that talents and preparation and experience and intelligence are not equal. But the linear model also contains a number of negatives. It encourages imitation rather than innovation.

We have to fit neatly into a box to get the job and keep the job. It doesn't recognize the diversity of talents we bring to any job and that problems can be solved and goals can be accomplished in many different ways. It can create a conformist culture that tries to fit everyone on the same ladder or in the same slot.

It's not a kind way of working. It often pits people against each other for a slice of the pie. Many get trampled in the scramble to the top. New thinking is lost. Visions are destroyed. And the ones who win may not be the best, but merely the toughest. But we were told this is how it is, this is how it always has been, this is how it always will be. We may as well get used to it and toughen up.

The web-thinking model

In the last twenty or thirty years, this competitive, linear model has been questioned. Archaeologists and anthropologists and historians have discovered an older model for working and living together, which is more like a circle or a spiral. The earliest societies were structured around a cave, a campfire, and a town square, and seemed to be more interactive rather than competitive. Some of these more circle-oriented societies seem also to have been more peaceful societies. One of the earliest, Catal Huyuk in Turkey, showed no evidence of war or violence for almost a thousand years.[82] It seems there were other workable models that might have advantages over the hierarchy.

As more women and others with diverse ethnic backgrounds have entered the workforce, they have brought other views of how best to achieve one's goals. Many who have been unhappy with the stresses of the competitive model have been seeking a new way of working that is more mutual, collaborative, and relational.

Although some have likened these alternative models to a circle or a spiral, I personally prefer the term "Web-Thinking", since this model is more complex. The term seems to have been created separately by two women – Sally Hegelson, who writes about business in *The Circle of Inclusion*, and Helen Fischer, an anthropologist who uses this term in *The First Sex*.

I became interested in this model because I felt there was something intrinsically non-spiritual about the linear model. It divided rather than unified. It forced us to see others as an adversary. It believed in scarcity rather than abundance. I spent some years trying to find an alternative model and to name it, and use it.

Web-thinkers believe we become successful, not by working *against* each other, but by working *with* each other. When we move from being linear thinkers to web-thinkers, we look for ways to collaborate with others to achieve a goal. We think in terms of teams, where each person is contributing something equally important to the success of any project, or mission, or business. Web-thinking recognizes that almost everything we do in our work demands cooperation with others and input from others.

As I write this book, I realize I'm relying on ideas from many people. My philosophy and theology of work and success has been formed by teachers, mentors, bosses, colleagues, clients and friends over many years. Take them away and I have nothing. Once I started on the undertaking of writing this book, my success was dependent on the work of others. The book wouldn't have been sold without the help of my agent. While writing the book, I have had the help of the interview subjects in the book, who come from all over the world, and readers who give me feedback as I write. The book needs the help of the team at the publisher who edit, print, and distribute and market the book. Although some might try to rate the importance of each one of the team, trying to determine who's important and who's not, the web-thinker has little interest in that kind of ranking. The group surrounding this book is a team. We don't rate the importance of each person as a hierarchy, deciding who is up and who is down on a ladder, because it doesn't seem to achieve the larger goal that we all want – a successful book.

Although our society might tell us who's the most important in any endeavor, identifying that person is not as easy as it might seem. Society might tell us the CEO is the most important, but where would that person be without workers, inventors, marketing people, sales people, and various technicians? And spiritual people have never used the world's ranking to determine who we respect and who we don't. We have other ways of thinking.

The Jesus approach

When I started studying the web-thinking model and using it in my own business, I was struck by how Jesus used the team approach, in spite of the fact that he easily could have declared himself as the Top of the Sky-High Ladder and the Best There Is!

When Jesus began his mission, what did he do first? He formed a group, a kind of team around him of twelve disciples. They didn't seem very skilled, nor important, but he must have seen something in them because they accomplished the objective well. The group expanded from twelve to about thirty people who followed him around the countryside. These included several women, including Mary of Magdala, Joanna, Susanna, and many others. It was undoubtedly a kind of ragtag group without official status, proper attire, and no classy modes of transportation. The group expanded again to more than seventy, and then again to hundreds and then thousands and then millions.

This ever-widening circle is one of the aspects of web-thinking. If you look at a spider's web, you can see there are concentric circles. Rather than one ladder that everyone has to fit on, and where there's only space for one person on each rung, the web ripples outward. There is room for many.

On a spider's web, the line is a line of connection, not of division. The line connects the outer circles and the inner ones. There are no boundaries, but the web continues to ripple outward, as far as the spider wants to reach. There are no ins and outs. Everything is related to everything else.

I turned to this model in the 1980s because I was desperate to make my career work. But I wanted something else. I wanted a happy work life, and I wasn't at all sure I could get it if I were looking over my shoulder all the time, wondering who was trying to pass me by.

I had tried to get my career going for almost fourteen years. I had plenty of degrees (at that time, a BA, two MA degrees, and a ThD) and had experience in my chosen field of drama – teaching at several colleges and a university, directing plays, and writing articles. Yet, nothing was working.

I thought someday I would become a self-made woman. But my lack of success isolated me and I saw many people as my competitors and therefore as people I had to be wary of. As a result, I couldn't form friendships within my chosen field of theater and then film. Yet, these were the people who were most apt to hire me, or recommend me for a job, or give me much-needed advice.

Finally I sat down one weekend and checked out every book I could find on women in business at the library, and proceeded to skim all the books to find some answer to what was wrong with me, or wrong with my way of thinking.

A light went off in my head when I read that many men have a business model that might look as if it's competitive, but is actually based more on a team-sports model. Guys play team sports, such as football and baseball and basketball. Although they are competitive with the other team, they aren't necessarily competitive among themselves. In fact, Vince Lombardi, the great coach of the Green Bay Packers (and a Roman Catholic from my home state of Wisconsin), was once asked why his team was so successful. He replied, "Teamwork is what the Green Bay Packers are all about. They didn't do it for individual glory. They did it because they loved one another."[83]

I began to understand the team model as a model of love, care, support, and shared knowledge. I tried to re-think my work in terms of a team model. I started asking myself, "Who do I need in order to do well?" Since I didn't have any mentors in the film business, nor did I know many people, I realized I had to start forming my own team. I hired a career consultant who had a profoundly inclusive way of looking at business. She recommended I also work with a marketing person, a publicist, a media consultant, a seminar consultant, and for those times when I appeared on television to promote my books, a clothes consultant. Although I had very little money, I made my team my first priority, and invested in them whenever I could.

I also decided the team members had to have two qualities – they had to be good at what they did, and they had to be supportive of me. I wanted good people on my team – people I could call when my work went well. People who would cheer me on and support my goals.

I then began to question the sports-team model, because it meant we could like each other on our own team, but had to be competitive with people from the other team. I wondered if maybe we could actually see others as team members as well, although, perhaps, further out on the spokes of our rippling web. I figured if we are all working toward the same big goal – of helping others and creating a better world – then anyone working toward that goal should be someone I could support. Even if that person has a similar business to mine, there's no reason for me to try to get in the way of them doing their good work and doing well.

Recognizing the gifts of others

Web-thinking recognizes the good things in life are abundant, not scarce. There is plenty of need in the world for our work and the work of others. The pie is much bigger than we might think.

Web-thinking also tries to discern the gifts of others, recognizing we bring many different gifts to the needs of the world. St. Paul recognized this when he said: "there are many different gifts, but it is always the same Spirit; there are many different ways of serving, but it is always the same Lord. There are many different forms of activity, but in everybody it is the same God who is at work in them all."[84] We are one body with many gifts. Just as the foot doesn't wonder why it's not a hand, and the hand doesn't wonder why it's not a head,[85] web-thinkers don't ask everyone to be alike. We all have work to do to contribute to a larger goal than just an egocentric goal of becoming better known, getting more business, selling more, and thereby having more things in life to make us more comfortable. We have bigger fish to fry than this!

Web-thinking as intrinsically spiritual

Web-thinking is known as a kinder model since it doesn't depend on nastiness or deception to find success.

Many of you reading this book may have felt that gut-wrenching insecurity that often comes when we think someone else is getting the better of us and getting the perks we think we deserve. Although we may be doing just fine, the success of another person makes our lives miserable and takes away the joy of our achievement. We feel their success can only mean our failure. We believe every time someone says another person is particularly wonderful, they're really saying we're particularly mediocre. Every plus the other person gets, we interpret as a minus for us.

We not only fear the success of others, but we applaud their failure, hoping to raise our level as a result. There's a word for this in German – *schadenfreude* – which means wishing for the failure of others and enjoying it when someone makes a mistake or has an accident. The literal translation is "damage joy". Yet what a terrible existence that sets up for us! Where is God and kindness and compassion and care and joy and peace in this kind of worldview?

Overcoming our feelings of competition

Competitive feelings are natural, especially since most of us have grown up in a world where that was the norm. We became enculturated into that way of thinking. It's normal to feel stuck in that mindset and wonder if we can escape it. But I believe we can.

About the time I began my business as a script consultant, another person in my field began giving seminars on screenwriting. He was very popular and known as a truly great teacher in the field. Many times my clients, or his students, would sing his praises to me. Every time I would hear the hymn to his greatness, I felt smaller, more uncertain, and felt a knot form in my stomach. I wanted my praises to be sung also, although some part of me recognized the problem wasn't whether someone was singing my praises or not (some were!), but the fact was, any praises to him felt as if they diminished me. Whether it was true or not, it was how I felt.

I didn't like this feeling and wondered if I could overcome it. Every time I felt that competitive gut-wrenching twist in my stomach, I began to stop and do a little prayer to try to get past it. I became determined I would not let this get the better of me because I recognized it would take away the joy of my work. I didn't want to go through my work life having enemies and wishing others ill.

It took almost ten years to get completely over that feeling of competition with him and with others. But it seemed absolutely essential, because once we get caught up in the competitive world, there will always be plenty of fodder to feed us. As other people became script consultants, or began to do seminars, they also began getting accolades which would reawaken that competitive feeling. When a colleague of mine jokingly called this the "seminar wars" and suggested the various consultants and seminar leaders have a party and get to know each other better, I felt threatened. I also believed he was absolutely right – it was time the wars stopped!

It took several more years before a group of us began to form our businesses on a collaborative web-thinking model. But, we did. And yes, we also eventually had that party, plus many more! By seeing colleagues as friends and allies, many of us who do similar work in the film industry now are part of each other's support system. We recommend each other for jobs, sometimes team teach and team consult, discuss contracts and problems with each other, endorse each other's books, rely on each other for advice and insight, and see each other as important people on each other's webs.

Our support of each other flows back and forth, giving and receiving. Instead of insecurity, we are bolstered up by others' belief in us and our talents. Instead of fear, we have a sense of peace and joy in our work. We are not isolated and alone, but connected.

Using web-thinking to change the world

Although churches and social-service organizations use many different models to make decisions about their social work and their relief work, some use a non-linear approach.

Historically, Quakers have used a consensus model for decision-making. Every decision that is made needs to find unity within the group. Decisions are not voted on, but the group reaches consensus about whether to follow one plan, or one course of action, or not.

Quakers believe this form of decision-making works because they believe the Holy Spirit leads us to unity, not to division. If a decision is right, the group wisdom and the group's ability to tune in and listen to the Spirit will lead them in good directions.

Of course, sometimes the group has difficulty deciding. The Clerk might then call for some moments of silence, to make sure someone's ego is not in the way of a decision, or to see if a third way emerges. Often new creative solutions come out of these quiet moments, as the stirring of the Spirit takes the group in some new directions.

Although this may seem like a very long process, many decisions are made more quickly than in the surrounding society. All Quakers reached consensus against slavery by the late 1700s, even though the United States didn't eradicate slavery for another hundred years. All Quakers agreed on equal rights, a century or more before women received the right to vote in America and other countries.

With consensus, there is no one in the group to sabotage a plan of action. When everyone is in agreement, everyone then works towards the same goal. There is no conflict or tension taking up energy or time. Everyone has been heard, and the group moves in the same direction.

Quaker Paul Whitehouse from England describes the Quaker Meeting for Business which is based on this model: "Meetings for church affairs, in which the Religious Society conducts its business, are meetings for worship based on silence, carrying the expectation that God's guidance can be discerned if members are truly listening together and to each other. The unity that is sought depends on the willingness of all to seek the truth in each other's utterances. There is no voting in the meetings, because the Religious Society believes this would emphasize the divisions between differing views and inhibit the process of seeking to know the right way forward, the will of God as expressed in the sense of the meeting. This model asks us to listen, to get our ego out of the way, and to seek the truth together." This model is also used at Meetings of the Board of Governors at Sidcot, an independent Quaker school, of which he is the chair.

Collaboration used in business

Although it may seem web-thinking would work well for smaller businesses, and for churches, or for social-service agencies, many believe it wouldn't work for a corporate structure. But that's not true. There are some good examples of businesses that use a more collaborative model and have achieved great success.

Some corporations, such as Saturn Cars, have created their businesses as a web model with small groups working together in marketing, manufacturing, sales, design, and so on. Other companies, both large and small, have used this model as a way of doing business.

One company that uses the non-linear model in business is the Scott Bader Company, which manufactures polyester composites and synthetic resins used in the marine, transport, construction and chemical industries. It is based in the UK, but now also manufactures in Dubai, South Africa, France and Croatia, and has distribution operations in the USA, Sweden, the Czech Republic and China.

It was originally founded by Ernest Bader in 1921, a Christian and a Quaker, who desired to base the business on Christian values and principles. The *Scott Bader Handbook* describes some of the principles which are the basis for the business. Bader believed "a world where capital employed labour was not sustainable; rather labour should employ capital to help eliminate social injustice and waste."[86] Bader believed capitalism had to be restructured, and wanted to create a company that not only created a good product, but served the world. He felt his company should take responsibility for creating a truly responsible society. It was dedicated to a spirit of cooperation and a goal to help eliminate social injustice and waste. In short, he wanted to use its business to help create a better world.

Sue Carter, the company's Commonwealth Secretary in the UK, describes the history of the business: "In 1951, Bader gifted the company to its employees. The share capital and therefore the ownership of the company was transferred, free of charge, to Scott Bader Commonwealth Limited ('The Commonwealth'), an organization created for that purpose with charitable status. This highly generous and imaginative act established a common trusteeship business. This means there are no external shareholders, which makes the company totally independent. The intention of the founders was to create a radical company, its well-being entrusted to those who work in it with democratic involvement. As a result the workers enjoy many of the benefits (and responsibilities) of ownership without the right to sell the business. The responsibilities, however, are key in that each generation must ensure the ongoing success of the organization so future generations can benefit from its continued existence."

Company literature explains how the company integrates its Christian principles and rethinks ideas in a variety of ways. It's committed to environmental issues, to developing new and improved products to minimize environmental impact, to innovation in the area of technology which allows their products to be ever more environmentally friendly. The company is committed to making reductions in the areas of greenhouse gas emissions, waste production and waste usage, and has set targets they hope to achieve within five or ten years. This approach has helped them be productive, and actually outperform many of their rivals.

The way the company judges success is based on Christian principles as well as profits. The *Handbook* says they judge their success, not just by profits, but by their honesty, their innovation, and their use of sustainable development principles. Part of the company's purpose is to "encourage the growth, development, health and well being of our people, who take a responsibility for their personal contribution." They ensure equality of opportunity and work toward "helping those less fortunate than ourselves by sharing our business success through money, time and effort."

Sue describes how profits are divided: "To fulfill its obligation to the wider community, there is the provision in the Articles of Association for the manufacturing company for the net profit to be divided as to a minimum of 60% for taxation and reserves, a maximum of 20% for staff bonuses provided at least the same amount is paid to the Charity. In reality, with the agreement of the workers more than 60% is retained in the business and there is a minimum annual payment to the Charity to honour its charitable commitments. Ernest Bader wanted to ensure that whenever staff benefited from a profit, they would share with those less fortunate. Several millions have been donated to charities which are recommended by the employees in each country. Some of the charities have included water for villages in Africa and India, health care clinics in South America and many projects for the homeless in the UK. At all locations, every effort is made to ensure any new construction complements the surrounding landscapes and takes account of the views of local residents."

As the company has grown, it has moved to a representative democracy based on the principle of a diffusion of power. It is governed to "ensure that no one group wields too much power at the expense of others."

Sue describes the management style: "The management style is open in which all people are freely accessible and accountable. First names are used throughout the organization – respect has to be earned rather than coming automatically with the position. They practise the principle of diffusion of power by holding informal discussions and consult widely on decisions that affect the people that work there, e.g. pensions; working conditions; investment; expansion. Wherever possible decisions are reached by consensus. The committees work closely together and involvement and teamwork is emphasized. Although this can take a longer time to reach a decision, it ensures that, once made, a new policy will be widely understood and effectively implemented. An example of this occurred when making changes in the pension in the UK policy which received 100 percent support following a protracted briefing and discussion stage. Finally, the structure also means managers are no better off than the staff as they are treated in the same way in relation to recognition and reward."

Workers at Scott Bader have a voice through their elected representatives and therefore can feel more involved. Those who become representatives do so in addition to their normal day-to-day role and they do so because they care about what happens to the company and about preserving the principles upon which it was founded.

Sue says: "Scott Bader is evidence that different business structures can work and are sustainable. However, the international business structure brings with it distinct challenges, particularly with regard to balancing the needs of the business and external pressures with the requirement to involve people in the decision making processes and adhering to the founding principles. Therefore the ongoing development and education of each generation of workers is essential."[87]

The web model can be the model of the future. It can also be a model for those who want to incorporate spiritual and democratic values into their work.

Questions for reflection and discussion

1. What has been your experience of linear competitive thinking? What parts were negative? What parts were positive?
2. How would you define the difference between linear and collaborative thinking? Have you used both? How have they worked?
3. In what way is web-thinking spiritual? Have you ever used this model?
4. What are the most difficult aspects of web-thinking to learn?
5. Why do you think Jesus chose disciples? How did they help him communicate and express his work?

Scripture to consider

Read the chapters about the calling of the disciples from Matthew 4, Mark 3, Luke 5. Read about the sending out of the 70 (sometimes 72) from Luke 10. Discuss how this represents the web-thinking model.

CHAPTER 7

Developing a Sense of Smell

The true Christian's nostril is to be continually attentive to the inner [and outer] cesspool.

C.S. Lewis

A number of years ago my friend Cathleen said to me, "Linda, you need to develop a sense of smell. You don't seem to notice the scoundrels and betrayers and people who are up to no good. You never noticed Mary's abuse, Jason's dishonesty, and Marilyn's crazy-making, even though several of us told you to 'watch out!' Start noticing. Start sniffing out the problems, or you, and your business, could be in trouble!"

All of us have encountered the negatives in our business, some more than others. Many good-hearted people have seen the bad things in their lives and business take a toll on their health, their relationships, their finances, and their ability to keep doing the work they love. Whether we call it "difficult people" or "Satanic forces" or "evil", the negatives have the potential to disrupt or stop our good work, to destroy our reputation, sap our energy, and to bring to ruin what has taken many years to build up. If we're not careful, the negatives can overcome the positives, and take away the joy we savor in the work we do.

Every business has some difficulties which may not be evil at all, but just part of the natural up-and-down processes of a business. This may be because of problems in the economy due to forces far beyond our control. Or a problem a supplier has in getting material to us, which slows down our work. Or problems which our client base encounters, which affect us. Or simply dreaming so big that the goal doesn't come easily. There is the natural rain that falls on any business.

But if we're doing good work, and working to manifest the Good and Holy Spirit within our world, it's natural for us to encounter evil in one form or another. Naturally there will be opposition and resistance to our work. We are na ve if we think all will flow well and all will be well.

Spiritual people tend to take three different approaches to these negatives. Some walk blithely into the woods, not seeing, or hearing, the wolf who often comes in disguise, but clearly is up to no good. Others have razor-sharp judgments and draw boundaries tightly, quick to notice anytime someone crosses a line or shows the smallest flaw in judgment. They label the slightest negative quickly and remove people from their life, even though they may have been loyal. The first hasn't developed any sense of smell. The other misidentifies danger where none exists, and is unable to see and hear where forgiveness is called for.

There are, however, those who have developed wisdom and discernment, who know the perfumed scent from a foul odor, and have developed an ability to deal with it.

Sniff out the good and the bad

There are those who say they can smell evil. They talk of the foul odor of the devil. They say some things really do smell to high heaven. They can smell when something is rotten with corruption. In the play, *Cat on a Hot Tin Roof*, Big Daddy talked about the odor of mendacity. In *The Fugitive*, US Marshal Sam Gerard walks out of the apartment of the killer. Although he has no proof the man has done anything wrong, he turns to his fellow Marshal and says, "This man's rotten!" Gerard simply knows it and feels it.

When some people are asked, "How do you know if it's God or the devil who has come calling?" they answer, "I can smell the difference. It's the ability to discern truth!" The touch of evil is often accompanied by a chill or coldness, an ability of some people to simply wipe others off the map – whether literally or figuratively – with no ability for empathy.

Dr. Douglas Millham from Kenya has developed a good sense of smell over the years: "I am a person drawn to crisis – to people, churches, groups, nations, tribes, families, who are fragile, hurting, vulnerable or wounded – where the presence of love, compassion, encouragement can assist in bringing these people to a transcendent and transforming moment of experiencing God's love, peace, and presence. Over the years, I've become an expert in reading people of all backgrounds, ages, cultures, reading their motives, actions, goals and discerning their ethics, values, integrity. Separating the followers of God from the fakers, the real from the pretenders, those who are manifestly hurting, the maneuverors from the manipulators, the simply misled from the truly evil and corrupt. This is a heavy burden and a tremendous gift in my profession – which is connecting the resources of a compassionate world with the needs of vulnerable children and communities."

Douglas knows there is true evil in the world, and his work demands he recognizes the traces of it, whether subtle or overt. Although most of us don't need to focus on it, we do need to be wise enough to see it for what it is. We need to learn to see the red flags. We need to teach our antenna to go up when something comes on our radar that isn't quite right. We need to get a whiff of the spoiled, corrupt stink of evil. It isn't enough to think that if we're just nice and loving, everyone will be nice and loving back, and if they're not, it's because we're not nice and loving enough. There are plenty of people in the world who will lie, betray, and do us wrong. Sometimes this is done through fear and insecurity and insensitivity. Sometimes negative people haven't developed their soul and have no other way of responding. Sometimes someone is simply out to get us, and we are astounded and agog at the creative manipulations they'll go through, seemingly immune from the consequences of their actions.

This is a spiritual matter, not just a matter of good and wise business practices. If we're taking too much time trying to interpret and forgive manipulative actions, chasing money owed to us, and trying to accommodate bad manners, anger, put-downs, and meanness, we aren't focusing on the work we're called to do. If we don't recognize evil when we see it, not only can it sabotage our work, but it can sabotage God's work as well.

British writer G.K. Chesterton put the call to develop a sense of smell into humorous verse in "The Song of the Quoodle":

They haven't got no noses,
The fallen sons of Eve
Even the smell of roses
Is not what they supposes;
But more than mind discloses
And more than men believe

They haven't got no noses,
They cannot even tell
When door and darkness closes...

The smell of snare and warning,
The smell of Sunday morning,
God gave to us for ours...

They haven't got no noses,
They haven't got no noses,
And goodness only knowses
The Noselessness of Man.

Developing a healthy sense of sin

We don't like to think about evil and sin. We tend to think that any discussion of the part we play in helping evil live and thrive gives us low self-esteem. It makes us seem imperfect at a time when we'd like to think we're doing everything right. Sin seems to be a rigid word, that lets people easily label others as wrong and keeps them focused outward, rather than having to look at themselves.

Although we may want to get rid of the word, if we don't develop a healthy sense of sin, we can easily get blind-sided. We can miss the clues and signs that tell us that something is not right.

There are many different definitions of sin – missing the mark, disobedience, not living up to our God-given potential, the actions we do that allow evil to continue to thrive.

There are many different ways of defining these evil forces. Mythologist Pamela Jaye Smith, author of the book, *The Power of the Dark Side*, defines three categories of evil. She says evil can be personal, impersonal, and suprapersonal. Pamela says: "The first, the personal, is our own psychological stuff – our Shadow, our phobias, our weaknesses, our prejudices. Too often we blame our failures on the indifference or wrath of the Deity, or the evil actions of the Dark One. Most often though, it's just us getting in our own way. It's more the Dim Side than the Dark Side. Then there are illnesses, stupidity, social ills, and spiritual dilemmas… all hold us back.

"Second is the Impersonal Dark Forces which are the natural forces that can create what seems to us humans to be evil. Earthquakes, floods, wildfires, volcanic eruptions, droughts, and diseases are impersonal and constant reminders that Nature is bigger than us and must always be taken into account.

"Third is the suprapersonal, the people and systems that purposefully do evil in the world, such as genocide, or use the personal failures of others to accomplish their heinous goals. This is often what we think of as true evil, which can be quite overwhelming and can threaten to overcome us."

Most of us will never encounter the big evils in the world – the ones clearly defined which we all recognize immediately. We probably will never be hijacked, or be in a concentration camp, or be the victim of murder or terrorism.

Yet, some people choose jobs that deal in one way or another with these large problems. Their work depends on their ability to name the evil and to then know how to deal with it. We can learn about the little evils by looking first at the big ones and at the ways people collude with evil.

For those who are working for social justice and trying to defeat the great destructive powers in the world, it's essential to understand these forces. Not noticing can be dangerous, and even fatal.

Tim Costello is the head of World Vision in Australia – a charity that works with poverty and justice issues. He says before we can confront evil, first we must name evil: "Christian faith doesn't detach from evil but knows evil is real. Evil has to be named. It has to be engaged. It has to be redeemed."

Tim puts evil into two different categories. The first is natural disasters which would be similar to Pamela's impersonal dark forces. Tim says: "You struggle to find language to explain this, other than that there is natural evil, savagery, cruelty, whether it's a tsunami, cyclone, earthquake, drought in Africa. It's unfair, capricious, and you can't reason with it.

"The other difficult category is human evil. Having been in Darfur, you can see the evil where political opponents are attacked in villages and refugee camps. This is human evil that is incomprehensible and overwhelming in its viciousness and savagery. It's mind-boggling in terms of the human capacity to inflict pain and suffering."

Sometimes the natural evils are compounded by

the inhumanity of those who have the ability to help. "In Burma (Myanmar) you had a natural disaster of the cyclone, but the political/institutional response has made it very difficult to get access to people and to save them. The political evil is about survival, control, and power so in Burma you're facing a natural disaster that helps human evil by setting up barriers, hurdles, responses that are evil. The natural disaster has turned into a human disaster. It's like the fox who attacked the vineyard and is now in charge of the vineyard."

For Tim, the consequences of both natural and human evil are pain, suffering, and the misuse of power.

Sister Luz, from the Good Shepherd Congregation, is the head of a charity called WODEEF (Women's Development and Earth Foundation) which works with the marginalized sector of women and children in both the rural and urban settings in the Philippines. She also sees identifying and trying to overcome the misuse of power as an important part of WODEEF's work. She defines evil as those actions that dehumanize us: "The Philippines has a long history, over 400 years, of colonization. This colonization has put into place dehumanizing structures handed down to generations during four centuries of exploitative and oppressive relationships between the powerful and the powerless. Evil is able to continue because of the ingrained culture and structures in our society. In the Philippines, there is the cultural heritage of *takot* and *hiya* (literally translated as 'fear and shame')."

Evil is further compounded because the powerful and the powerless continue to play their roles. "Most of us Filipinos are either afraid or ashamed to do what is right and to speak up for our rights or for what we believe. Much more so with the marginalized. They are used to being told what to do and to be dependent on those above them."

As Sister Luz says, some of these evils are ingrained into our society. They are not just individual, but they are social, political, and structural.

James Okuk has been in the middle of the war in the Sudan and sees the tragedies and evil daily. He defines other evils, particularly those that have raged in his country: "War is always ugly whether waged for a defense or an offense. The victors may praise it but they cannot escape its destructiveness, trauma and ruins. The victims regret it and thirst for its vengeance. War has no home; the displacement of individuals and families becomes an unavoidable consequence. War is an enemy of human dignity and environmental safety."

Missionary Lisa Borden from Tanzania says, "I'm on a continent rife with disaster, war, disease, poverty, corruption and abusive leadership (to mention a few). These disasters are further compounded because anyone who comes to help can easily fall into despair. Evil prevails because it seems too overwhelming.

"There is also the sense of hopelessness that can quickly overtake you in Africa. People find themselves wondering how their small effort can be of any use in the face of the tidal wave of suffering across the entire continent. Many people come to Africa 'to help' and find themselves soon overwhelmed by the circumstances they face. They have 'sacrificed' to come and 'serve', yet they find the corruption of local officials blocking their every attempt to assist the very endeavors these officials should want to see succeed. Whether they are building schools or homes for orphans or training people in life skills or caring for the terribly ill, they can feel obstructed by endless red tape or the demands made upon them to bribe their way into being 'allowed' to proceed or feel hurt and disillusioned when their home is robbed by their own neighbors.

"The overwhelming nature of evil and suffering and pain can stop you in your tracks", says Lisa. "For instance, there will soon be 40 million orphans on this continent. Where do you even begin?"

We can find these dehumanizing actions and structures throughout the world, whether we're in a First, Second, or Third World country. They come in many forms and if we learn to recognize them, we can better deal with them. War, terrorism, imprisoning the innocent, and the many ways that one person or group objectifies another, can be found in all societies. Sometimes these evils come in the form of discrimination – racism, sexism, ageism, classism – all of which keep us from having an equal opportunity to do what we feel called to do. Oppression, in any form, whether overt or subtle, holds us down, limits us and can kill both body and spirit.

According to Protestant theologian Paul Tillich, sin can be defined as alienation. Rather than pulling us together in our shared humanity, it separates us. We come out of the harmony of the Garden of Eden into a world of alienation from God, from ourselves, and from each other.

Tillich analyzes part of the Garden of Eden story as separation from our work. When Adam is cursed, it is his ability to do his work harmoniously that is cursed: "Cursed be the soil because of you! Painfully will you get your food from it as long as you live. It will yield you brambles and thistles, as you eat the produce of the land. By the sweat of your face will you earn your food."[88] No longer will the earth willingly give him a harvest. His work will no longer be joyous and natural, but will now be difficult. There will be barriers to productivity.

For Lisa and James, Tim and Sister Luz, their work revolves around confronting these barriers to harmony and trying to empower the alienated. They see, constantly, individual, social and political attitudes and actions that squelch many people's spiritual gifts and their ability to offer them.

Confronting the troublemakers and the trouble

Few of us work within the areas of social justice, and thereby few of us daily confront the big sins that shout at us about great human suffering. But sin can also be subtle and difficult to discern, especially in its early stages when it may cloud judgment or begin to simmer underneath the surface until it explodes. Some of these little problems may just seem like simple unimportant irritants.

Yet, it's these small things that need to also be labeled, since they're the ones most of us will confront in our work. Very few of us (and probably no one reading this book) are murdering or embezzling in order to further our careers. Very few steal. Only a few sleep their way to the top. Some may be a bit greedy or envious or cheat a bit, perhaps stealing paper clips or cheating on their taxes. But these seem like such minor sins when compared to the massive suffering in Darfur, the murders in Kenya, the human rights abuses that exist in many countries in the world.

Yet, look at the focus on the sins in the Bible. Why

does the Bible so often harp on about what seem to be the petty little things – backbiting, malice, nastiness, deceit, strife, whisperings, murmurings, slander, spitefulness, anger, guile, lying, mocking, complaining, hypocrisy, quarrelling, dissension, jealousy, selfish ambition?[89]

With all the big problems in the world, why do so many of the wise writers in the Old and New Testaments continually talk far more about these seemingly little things? Jesus takes these things seriously and has some strong words to say about the subtle oppressions that the powerful often inflict. So do Paul and Peter and John, and the wise writer of Proverbs. And how is this relevant to us, who are basically decent folk, doing a reasonably good job? What's the big deal if a little bit of envy or a bit of malice and egocentricity creeps into our work? What are the sins we need to sniff out in ourselves, and in the people we work with? And why do they matter so much?

C.S. Lewis, one of the most respected Christian writers, says: "The sins of the flesh are bad, but they are the least bad of all sins. All the worst pleasures are purely spiritual: the pleasure of putting other people in the wrong, of bossing and patronizing and spoiling sport and back-biting, the pleasures of power, of hatred. For there are two things inside me competing with the human self which I must try to become. They are the Animal Self and the Diabolical Self. The Diabolical Self is the worse of the two. That is why a cold, self-righteous prig who goes regularly to church may be far nearer to hell than a prostitute." And then he adds, "Of course, it is better to be neither."[90]

This is strong language – from both the Bible and from theologians such as Lewis. But there's a reason for them taking these other sins very seriously. Proverbs compares "the dripping of a gutter on a rainy day" to a quarrelsome woman, and clarifies the problem: "whoever can restrain her, can restrain the wind, and take a firm hold on grease."[91] It is the continual dripping which chips away at us. Our work gets corrupted by the drip, drip, drip that can inhabit our daily world. It's not usually the big lies, but the little falsehoods, the mischief, the perversion of the truth that sow problems. It can be a feeling of betrayal in our gut that won't let up, and bothers us day by day as we rethink the incident and try to figure out what we, or he, could have done differently. It's the negative energy of a co-worker that erodes everyone's work. It's the innuendos that can cause a ripple effect outward from us toward others. Some remain small, and simply eat away at us. Others come to a very slow boil.

An old English proverb describes these small neglects:

> For want of a nail, the shoe was lost,
> For want of a shoe, the horse was lost,
> For want of a horse, the soldier was lost,
> For want of a soldier, the battle was lost,
> For want of a battle, the kingdom was lost.

Literature and film and the daily newspapers are filled with stories about such little sins. In Shakespeare's *Othello*, Othello and Desdemona die as a result of a few innuendoes and the misinterpretation of a handkerchief.

There are many verses in the Bible that talk about the consequences of these seemingly petty problems – a broken and wounded spirit,[92] a heavy and discouraged heart.[93] These little things immobilize us and waste our talents.

Individual resistance and opposition

On an individual level, most of us have met resistance and obstacles in our work. Much of it comes from the normal human flaws of others. People don't deliver on time. They need an extension in order to pay us. They make mistakes because of a lack of knowledge or a lack of caring. They discover they under-bid on a job and it's taking more time and resources than they had allocated, so now they're dragging their feet. They have other priorities than the work they're supposed to do.

Some of the lack of harmony in our work comes from our own weaknesses. We're pushed for results and we can't get results fast enough. We don't have the energy needed for a task. We don't have the preparation to know how to do something well and quickly. We might spend more time schmoozing with the client than is necessary and then are rushed to perform the actual job.

Many of us don't know some aspect of our work. We might be very good at the technical parts of our job, but not very good at the marketing or management parts. We might be terrific at the sales part of the job, but not at the bookkeeping part. Knowing our weaknesses and our strengths, and how our weaknesses can cause problems for us, and for others, helps us address what we have to learn.

Since no one is a villain in their own eyes, we can spend enormous amounts of energy blaming others rather than solving the problem. Or, conversely, we can always blame ourselves when something's going wrong and become paralyzed by self-criticism.

Although some of these sins seem to have deeper repercussions than others, any opposition can keep workers from doing what they're called to do, which separates them from the joy of their work and their potential to further build up the Kingdom of God.

Is it really such a big problem?

I have been fortunate in my own work to have a fairly smooth-flowing job. As a result, I tend to think these little sins are my own problem and I'm just taking them too seriously. But as I've thought about Paul's description of sins, I've begun to feel maybe they are worth looking at more closely, even if they seem so minor.

I chose to begin my own business because of a few experiences where I could see the eroding power of office politics and realized I didn't know how to play the game. I began to see the difficulties of working side by side with co-workers who wanted to step on my work to try to gain some advantage. And I began to see the problem which many people encounter in their work. Often they don't hate their job, but hate the people they have to work with who cause great stress for them every day.

Sometimes these problems get the better of us out of our own innocence. I have often ignored that little zing that occasionally awakens me and says, "Watch out! Look what's happening here. Notice what he, or she, is doing!" I have often smelled when something was beginning to rot, but then ignored the subtle odor, figuring it was nothing worth paying attention to.

In my twenties and early thirties, I taught college. I loved teaching, loved my students, and had many students affirm my ability as a teacher. In one job, however, I noticed a new co-worker seemed to be far more political than I was, and spent much time making sure she was an insider with all the powers-that-be. She would blithely go off to lunch with the Dean, and have long talks with the head of the department, and I kept wondering what was going on and what I was supposed to do about it. It wasn't that there was anything wrong with her having lunch with the Dean, but I suspected something else was going on besides a nice friendship. However, I was not skilled at discernment or understanding.

By the end of the year, I was let go from my job, along with several others in the department. I later learned that in these many talks she was dropping a sentence here, a sentence there, about me that set me up for my dismissal. I heard she had mentioned to the Dean, several times, that I would probably be quitting at the end of the year to get married because the man I was dating was getting his PhD and he'd get a job somewhere else. This wasn't true. I wasn't engaged, the man I was dating was still a few years away from his PhD, marriage wasn't being discussed, and there was always the possibility we'd stay in the area, even if we did get married.

I heard she made a comment to the head of the department about a question I couldn't answer in one of my classes and I later learned she would add a little laugh to these innuendos, as if her little comment was insignificant and a bit silly but cute, while implying I didn't know my subject well. She finagled and sidled and dripped politics. By the end of the year, she and the head of the department were the only ones left in what had been a six-person department (with some who were part time). By the next year, I learned that the head of the department was let go and she became head of the department. It took me some months to put everything together and to ask enough questions to figure out what had happened. And I decided it was time for me to get some understanding of the weasels of the world.

These small actions ripple outward. All six of us had to find other jobs quickly, since we were let go at the end of the school year. I was unemployed for three months, getting small unemployment checks from the government and trying to figure out a way to keep my apartment. At that point, another teaching job was out of the question. It was simply too late to pursue that. I finally got a job that paid very little, so my parents subsidized me every month while I was trying to figure out my next steps, but the new job then ended within a few months. I lived on the edge for the next five years, trying to find a new career since my research told me that continuing to teach drama in college was not a good option, especially after having been let go from a university job.

The head of the department, although retirement age, was forced to retire long before he felt ready to. Others left teaching and decided it wasn't worth the political maneuvering they had encountered.

Such innuendos may seem harmless at the time, but they can then grow into full-blown lies. Her seemingly small actions had political and social impact, as well as an individual impact. She lied, pure and simple, for her own advantage.

What are the steps for confronting evil?

We might think the bad things in life are beyond our ability to deal with them. But there are a number of techniques we can use when it seems the negatives are overwhelming our work.

First, recognize it

If there are problems that are keeping our work from flowing, recognize them as soon as possible. When we blindly go our merry way, the problems grow. Sin is subtle and the ability to discern a problem in its early stages is a sign of wisdom. Listen and look. Many of the sin makers in our world will tell us how honest they are, and insist they're people of integrity, but look at what they do, not what they say. I've noticed how often the most deplorable people are convinced they're wonderful, and I now always have a red flag go up when someone tells me about how honest they are. If they can't prove it, then don't believe it!

This might be as simple as recognizing we have a feeling about a client, a boss, or a colleague that something is not going right. It smells "off". We might get a sniff of a clue because we don't trust the person. We might be tempted to wonder why we're being so judgmental or untrusting, but it might be our sense of smell is right on. Or the person might do something nasty and unfair. It stinks and we're shocked by it. They might try to justify it, or even apologize, and we try to be nice about it and forgive and forget. But just because they said, "I'm sorry" doesn't mean they might not do it again.

Or a situation in our businesses might be causing us problems – whether there's not enough business coming in, or a problem with someone we work with, or our business may have grown too fast and we're trying to tell ourselves everything will turn out fine. Yet, if we're worried, we need to recognize the worry. Don't ignore the clues that say something may be wrong. Notice if someone won't let you criticize them or their policies. Notice if someone is bullying or suppressing others. Be aware whether your colleagues are trying to solve a problem or simply maintain their position.

Affirming our intuition is particularly important for people who work with social and political issues. They, in particular, need to trust their instincts. Every evil in the world has a root cause. We may not always be able to know exactly what it is, or to understand the many complicated elements that all come together to create an explosive situation, but there is still a catalyst that has started the march to malevolence. The sooner we can see it and deal with it, the better.

Respect that whiff that tells you something is not quite right, something is burning in the distance, there's something rotten in the vicinity. Even when there doesn't seem to be actual and apparent proof that your intuition is correct, there's a good chance the subtle whiff is there, in the air, and it's real. Sometimes we're wrong, but it's a good start to simply think, "I have a funny feeling about this person or this situation."

Ask yourself, "What is my part in this problem?"

We may become good at sniffing out the sins of others, but we also need to know our part in problem-making and how that affects our work. Our sins – whether attitudes or actions – affect others negatively. Our egos and the manipulation we do to keep ourselves in the forefront can cut off the contributions of others.

Although we may be well-intentioned, we can easily be tempted by the bright lights of the world and the promises that tell us we can get and keep whatever we want, if we only are willing to do a bit of compromising. These temptations can easily corrupt and taint our work and raise unrealistic expectations that if we follow the side streets and dark alleys, it will lead to all good things.

We need to take responsibility for our part in creating or maintaining the problem. We all have inabilities and blind spots in our lives and in our business.

We might ask, "Is this an individual problem with me, a business/management problem, or a social or political problem? Am I getting egocentric, or being unfair, or untruthful?" We start by cleaning up our own act. Then we look at the other problems and people who might be operating negatively.

Analyze the problem

Not every problem in our business comes from evil. Sometimes we identify something as bad, when it's actually just part of the step-by-step process toward success which isn't going as fast as we want it to go.

A business or management problem might be an inability to hire, or fire, an employee, even when it's necessary, or time management problems, or budgetary problems or an inability at some aspect of our business, such as public speaking or doing the books or writing reports.

A social or political problem might involve the culture. We might have a product ahead of its time, or perhaps behind the times, or we might come up against discrimination, or be part of office politics or a larger political agenda. Any of these, although they seem beyond the scope of our business, might still affect us.

We can apply the tests that Tim, Lisa, Sister Luz, and James use in order to discern whether the problem is a natural part of business or some evil we should confront: Is it a natural or human disaster? Do we feel overwhelmed, disillusioned, hopeless or hurt by these problems? Is it dehumanizing or oppressive? Does it offend human dignity?

And we can ask, "Where is it coming from?" Some of our problems come from ourselves, but some also come from unjust laws, cultural biases, and social inequalities.

Tim Costello says discernment demands analysis. We can apply his analysis working with the great evils of our world to the smaller, but significant sins we encounter in our work. Tim says, "We need a range of understanding and some political and social analysis to understand the dimensions of evil. We might need to analyze: Who has power, who doesn't? Who's getting what they want at the expense of others? How are some people standing on the shoulders of the misery of others to maintain their power, their greed, their wanton lust?

"We need to analyze the spiritual dimension as well to see what's in the human heart. We know humans have a capacity for good and a capacity for evil, so we need to understand how human nature can be corrupted. What cripples the human instinct for compassion and solidarity and how is that attitude woven into the systemic abuse of other humans?"

Mythologist Pamela Jaye Smith discusses the lure of evil that can cripple our human instinct for goodness.

She says, "Too often in business situations we're urged to fudge the numbers, hold back information that might influence a client or customer decision, cover up for a colleague's or boss's mistake. Very few businesses are truly guided by top-to-bottom integrity, regardless of what their vision statements says. Our basic tendency toward good can be subverted with the initial bite of compromise or calumny, then the denial to ourselves or our God, the larger crime, the cover-up, the grip of guilt, giving up any remaining inclination to do good, hardening the heart, and then just embracing evil."

Tim looks at the big picture of evil. "As a Christian, I have been dwelling on the idea of Paul's discussion of principalities and powers and spiritual wickedness in high places. Those principalities and powers have to be discerned and named. The normal categories that are good, such as government, family, and work, can all be corrupted and become demonic, and it's spiritual discernment to understand how they're fulfilling their purpose or whether they're acting in a crippling and arbitrary manner. All of these can be used to deceive and lie and oppress. All of these can be restraining or redeeming."

If necessary, make new policy

Most businesses have a number of policies they follow: "Pay up front." "Refund money if the person is dissatisfied with the product." "Always check the customer's ID." "Don't loan more money than the customer can afford to repay." Sometimes when problems come along, it's simply because the policy is not working. If someone continually finds customers don't pay the last installment, it's time to change the policy. If a business is constantly cheated by bad checks, it's time to change the policy. If we have constantly been gypped or cheated, it's time to recognize that not everybody is fair and just, and we need to run our businesses to take human flaws into account.

When I started my business, my clients paid when the work was finished. I then began to notice how often clients forgot their check-book, or said they'd pay later when their paycheck came in, or just didn't have all the money. I felt victimized and overwhelmed by this and spent countless hours trying to figure out how to get paid. I then called my career consultant who said, "It's time to change policy!" We changed my policy so clients paid half when they sent the script and half when the work was finished. But again, I noticed many had excuses for not paying the last half. I changed my policy again – now clients pay the full amount when they send me the work. I didn't want to be a bill collector. I wanted all of my energy to be put into the work itself.

If necessary, disconnect and disengage from the source of the problem

Out of our desire to be nice, forgiving, and kind, we can often get entangled with the wrong kind of people. We keep trying to change ourselves, rather than identify what hasn't worked, isn't working, and won't work. This can be done amiably and diplomatically, but we don't need the negative people in our lives. It's not good for us and it's not good for our work.

This doesn't mean blaming the person, or treating the person as an enemy. James Okuk says, "I try not to think and feel that I have enemies. From my meditation, I discovered that the moment I think and feel about some people as enemies, that's the moment I get worried of what they are planning to do against me. In most cases my worries do not come true. But by the time I realize this, my energy has already been exhausted by the illusion I had put myself in. Based on this experience, I made it a rule not to think of any person as an enemy. This positive thinking has helped me a lot to use my feelings and reasoning for better things in life that liberate me from the past 'big negatives'. Above all it made me be calm and patient in dealing with critical issues and fragile situations. This serenity has helped me to forge better ways ahead through harmonizing rather than conflicting with people."

Although we strive for harmony, sometimes we do have to limit or stop our relationship with a person. This doesn't mean we always have to let the other person know we're disengaging. We simply no longer make any effort to pursue the relationship. Other times, we have to make it clear we're disconnecting. In most cases, this can be done with kindness. We can recognize the human cost to our disconnecting – whether it means we fired someone and need to help them over the hump while they are looking for the next job, or whether it means we no longer do business with them but let them know we won't stand in their way. In all business dealings, there always needs to be room for compassion and understanding.

Sometimes, we also have to recognize we are not the only ones who might need to disengage from someone who is truly evil. We may need to warn others who are involved with them to be careful. It isn't gossiping and it isn't holding a grudge to say something to others, to let them know trouble could come their way. It's our duty, out of our integrity, to recognize the potential problem for others. We may need help from our spiritual community to recognize the difference between what is merely negative and problematical versus that which is evil. It's important we discern the difference.

Above all, forgive

Forgiveness doesn't mean we return to the old ways of being or doing. Just because we forgive someone doesn't mean we take them back into the fold and continue to do our business with them in the same way we did it before. It does mean we wipe away the negative feelings and any anger or resentment we have toward them. We allow ourselves to open our hearts toward them and recognize the possibility of change. Some will change. Some won't. But whatever their choice, we bear them no ill will.

Sometimes it helps to write a letter of forgiveness, not only to free them from our negative feelings but to free ourselves. We may, or may not, send it. After carrying around negative feelings about the teacher from the university who was partly responsible for me losing my job, I decided to write her a letter which I did send to her. Although my innocence was my main fault, I confessed to my innocence, wished her well, and decided I no longer wanted to carry around resentment. It helped me and it seemed to connect with her humanity, since she wrote back an honest and kind reply.

James Okuk sees that we begin this process when we look to the future, not the past. He says, "Evil comes easily into our lives when we allow the past to overshadow the future within the steps of our present life. Do not delve in the past but learn from it to forge a better path for the future. Most of our fears come from our reference to the past. Most of our hopes come from our strong belief in what the future holds for us. Most of our success comes when we liberate ourselves from the prisons and failures of the past. The regrettable past doesn't repeat itself in the present, neither can it project itself into the future when we have critically and sincerely learned our lessons from it.

"When you are surrounded by tragedies, be calm, cautious and keen to find a way out as quickly as possible, using the available means. Suspend the blame and deploy your energy exhaustively for a way forward rather than the way backward. Strengthen your hope for a better solution. Do not permit hatred or a sense of defeat to take hold of you when you happen to differ with others, or when they mistreat you."

Above all, remember to love, even when this is difficult. James says, "From my experience of tragedy, I came to know that love is more helpful than hatred. You do not get hurt by loving someone and wishing good things to the people who are against you. You feel in love with yourself when you love the people. But when you hate people, you feel even more internal suffering and hurt than them. Every time I find myself at odds with someone, I remind myself with this simple statement: 'No human being is an angel; neither can any human person be a devil.' I get calm when I meditate on this and then I let the anger go. I just say to myself after this reminder: 'If I do not love the people who hate me, then it is better for me not to be a Christian.' I find it hard to think of not being a Christian, and so I submit to the simple law of love of every human person whether he/she is friendly or hostile."

Use your clout for good

With success comes a certain amount of power and clout. It may be, for many of us, that part of our calling includes using our clout to help remove the limits and oppression that may affect others, even if it doesn't directly affect us. Even in small ways, we can work for individual and social justice. It can be part of God's saving work that as we become more successful, our good works ripple outward in many different ways.

Tim Costello believes it's important we expand our ideas of what it means when God saves. "As a Christian growing up, I often heard the question, 'Are you saved?' In the Bible, redemption works on many levels. It's not just a spiritual reality – although it is that for sure. It's also political – the slaves cried out for God and God said 'I will be your redeemer' and God liberated them from slavery. Redemption is economic – have the people the means of an income, a livelihood? Redemption is social. In the story of Ruth and Boaz, Ruth had no rights, no citizenship, and Boaz was a landowner who married her so there was social redemption. The whole earth is groaning for redemption on many levels – economic, political, social, environmental, spiritual."

Those who work in social-service jobs have a tremendous potential to change things for the better. Sister Luz sees transformation of individuals and society in her work. "In WODEEF, the economic empowerment projects are crucial to the transformation of the participating women. The process they undergo in the different micro-economic enterprises we sponsor is a sifting mechanism. The women who persevere are determined to improve the economic status of their families (without being dependent) and unknowingly the women then change themselves during the process, in many ways for the better."

It might also be part of our calling to speak out against injustice. Those who are successful are in a better place to do this than those who aren't. Although we may think we might lose a job or hurt our businesses by doing so, I have found most people respect the times I've spoken out, if I do it diplomatically. More than once I've offered to help negotiate some tensions between producer and writer. Or to help negotiate a conflict in a seminar or consulting situation.

I began speaking out shortly after I wrote my book *When Women Call the Shots: The Developing Power and Influence of Women in Television and Film*. I began to see part of my calling included working toward equality for women, which meant equality for myself but also for my female colleagues. Shortly after the book was published, I was asked to speak at a screenwriting conference. I noticed I was asked at the last minute, after the program was already published. I also noticed all the other eight speakers were men, even though there were a number of excellent women speakers in my field. I said "yes" to the invitation. At the conference, several women came up to me and said they had asked the men in charge why I wasn't invited, and the men said, "We forgot about Linda! Of course she should have been asked!" I realized the problem of inequality isn't always personal. I just wasn't on their radar because I didn't look like the guys.

I then analyzed the area of speakers at seminars and realized most of the people traveling abroad to give seminars were men, even though a number of women were equally qualified. I also realized if this were to change, I was the only person who could change it, since I was the only woman in a group of about eight people giving international seminars. I decided I would try to change this and wondered how quickly it could be done.

I began to let all the hosts of my seminars know about my female colleagues. They were happy for the information and began inviting them. I gave my female colleagues emails and contact information for the hosts I had in the past, and encouraged them to write them and let them know about their work, using my name as a reference.

I set the goal of equalizing the field, which meant there would need to be eight women traveling abroad since that's how many American men were giving international seminars. It only took two years to achieve this goal and now the numbers have remained just about equal.

But I also didn't want to only help women, since I have many good male colleagues, and began to recommend them as well. When I was asked to put together a team for seminars, I made sure there were both men and women on the team. I also noticed most of these seminar leaders are Caucasian, except for one speaker who is Asian-American whom I have recommended for a number of jobs. I am now looking for opportunities to recommend an African-American colleague of mine who is excellent and I'm trying to be aware of other speakers in my field who come from other ethnic backgrounds.

Using our clout often means consciousness-raising for each of us, and it takes courage to step out on behalf of others. But if we're doing the saving work of God, then we need to look for ways to expand our understanding and actions to help save others. This can work in many ways. When I feel competitive with others, and I want the job which means they won't get it, I often think, "I want everyone to be able to earn a living, and to do well. I don't want to do anything that gets in the way of someone having equal rights with me." Yes, I might still get the job, or the other person might, but I don't want to make anyone's life difficult by what I do or say.

I expect all of us have opportunities in our work to try to change some of the limiting social structures which can keep others from being able to contribute their gifts. This does not mean becoming a shouting and demanding activist who gets huffy at various slights, or self-righteous about their work, but it may mean taking the opportunity and becoming sensitive to how the issues of injustice and oppression affect others in your field.

Becoming wiser

Developing a sense of smell means developing our sensitivity to others and their situations, developing our intuition, developing our ability to discern the good from the bad, and developing wisdom.

Lisa says: "We should become wiser as we become more successful. I believe wisdom and success go hand in hand because success implies you have learned wisdom along the way and you're now applying that wisdom, which is, in turn, bringing you into more success. I'm not sure you can have one without the other.

"We need to learn to trust our instincts as well as our tried and true teaching or training. As Christians, we can expect God will answer our prayers for wisdom and assist us with his Holy Spirit who whispers to us. The book of Proverbs is entirely a handbook of practical wisdom, which tells us God wants to give us wisdom. And the New Testament promises in James 1:5: 'If any of you lacks wisdom, he should ask God, who gives generously to all... and it will be given to him.' And we need to expect intuition to be encouraged by his Spirit.

"Finally, the most obvious way to develop a sense of smell is to develop my relationship with God. The more I know him, the easier it is to recognize the sometimes subtle differences between what is truly good and what is not. As I grow in being a child of the light, I can see the difference between light and darkness more readily and clearly."

Questions for reflection and discussion

1. What are the negatives you've had to confront in your own work? What is their source? Would you consider them evil, or simply coming from your lack of knowledge or preparation?
2. Have you encountered any social evils in your work – where the problems you're facing don't come from you but from a social or cultural bias against you or your work? What is that bias? How does it work?
3. Have you been able to confront evil or overcome evil in your work? How did you accomplish that? What advice would you give others about it?
4. What have you learned about forgiveness and discernment through the process of dealing with the big, and small, sins in your own work?

5. Have you been able to make any social change by using your clout and power for the benefit of others? What happened? What obstacles did you confront? How did it work out?

Scripture to consider

Read the story of Jesus' temptation in the desert (Matthew 4; Luke 4). What were the temptations he encountered? How would giving in to these temptations have affected his work? In what way were his temptations similar to the temptations that you have encountered? Have you experienced any temptations of food, money, fame and respect, or power?

Read the Bible verses that speak of "the little sins" – such as in James 3, Romans 2, Colossians 3, etc. Why do you think Paul and other early Christian writers were so concerned about these sins? How did they affect the work of the early church? How do they affect your work?

CHAPTER 8

Where Do You Feel the Rhythm?

A bit of musicality, please!

From the film, Strictly Ballroom

In the Australian film, *Strictly Ballroom*, Scott Hastings wants to win the Pan-Pacific Ballroom Dance Championship, but he's too original, too creative with the steps. He's not "strictly ballroom." As a result, his long-time partner leaves him a short time before the competition. Forced to quickly find a dance partner, he begins dancing with Fran – who's not very good, is a kind of ugly duckling, but very willing to learn. He soon learns Fran's father and grandmother know how to dance, and have a few things to teach him. In one scene, the grandmother asks Scott, "Where do you feel the rhythm?" He begins moving his feet, and Grandma says, "No! *Aqui.* Here," and she taps his heart. "Listen to the rhythm. Don't be scared!" and she encourages him to dance from his heart.[94]

Scott didn't understand the relationship between the internal and the external, the inner and the outer, the nurturing heart and the responding body. We can only do truly great work when we pay just as much attention to what is happening within us, as we do to developing our physical and mental abilities and specific outward skills.

Like Scott, we can easily mistake the source of our rhythm. We can get confused about where to put our focus. We might wonder why St. Paul says "pray constantly"[95] and easily can decide it's a metaphor and he didn't really mean it that way. But Paul recognized his very important outer work was dependent on the connections which he established daily with his inner life. He was probably really telling us: "Connect with the Source, constantly! Allow your relationship with God to become so much a part of you, you are constantly aware of and in communion with the Holy Spirit." But how? And why is it so important?

What are you doing? Who are you being?

When I was a senior in college, I spent a Thanksgiving vacation with my aunt in Denver. My cousin Miriam was also visiting. Miriam was a few years older than I was and the daughter of a minister from the Evangelical Free Church. One morning I came down to breakfast and saw Miriam sitting in a chair.

I asked her, "What are you doing?"

"I'm reading the Bible."

I looked more closely and could see a Bible open on her lap. I was a little bit confused. "Oh! Why?"

"It's what I do every morning," she answered.

"Oh."

In my religious world, we went to church, heard the Bible read in church, read and discussed it in Bible Study, but something else was going on here. Miriam was having morning devotionals. We never did that. None of my friends ever did that. How interesting! How fascinating!

A few months later, I decided I needed to start a spiritual search, to move my religion from church-going and the occasional reading of a spiritual book to something much more personal. I began attending a Bible Church with an acquaintance, Wendy. One evening I knocked on Wendy's dorm door. She said "Come in" and I went into the room, but it was all dark except for a candle burning, and Wendy was sitting on the floor next to the candle.

"What are you doing?" I asked.

"I'm just sitting here watching the candle!"

"Why?"

"I'm meditating," said Wendy.

"Oh!"

I had never seen anyone just sit. Just be. I was an extrovert. A Type-A personality. We did things. We acted. We made things happen. We never just sat in silence. I was fascinated.

I soon realized I had a very undeveloped inner life. I began reading books, taking classes, learning to meditate (not easy for an extrovert), and within a few years joined the Society of Friends (Quakers), who believe in the necessity of silence and quiet to integrate our quiet reflective lives with a more spirit-filled active life.

The inner and the outer

There are many different ways of defining this relationship between the inner, introspective, reflective life, and the outer, external, active life. Some think of the inner life as the still waters, the quiet, peaceful, beautiful scene which we go to before moving into the frenzy of our daily life. We go there to rest up, to breathe deeply, and we sometimes think of it as a kind of vacation away from the hustle and bustle and noise of our daily life. Some go to this quiet place daily and some do retreats to spend a few days or a week there, and then move back into the activity of their lives. Most of the time this quiet place is visualized as a beautiful place in nature with birdsong and the quiet lapping of water and a gentle breeze.

Others visualize this relationship in musical terms. They feel they've got off rhythm or lost their rhythm, and they need to quiet down in order to get back in tune, to refind the melody and harmonies of their lives.

I like the musical metaphor because we start the melody in our quiet time, but allow the melody to continue through our active time. Instead of having two different times which we neatly put into categories – my quiet time, my active time – they begin to blend and connect and relate to each other. They might still be separate times, but each influences the other.

When we venture on the path to success, there is always the tendency to focus on one over the other. We can become so action-oriented that we become frenetic, always doing activities without taking the time to listen to where we're being led. This leads to wasted effort, wasted energy, and often taking wrong turns. Others simply meditate on what they are to do, but take no steps to do it simply because they're uncertain and afraid and are waiting for the big push, rather than the little nudge. We expect to find God in the thunder and the lightning, and instead find God in the still small voice that takes careful listening.

Nurturing both our faith and our action takes

spiritual discipline. If we don't take time to pray, to center, to let the things of the world settle somewhere else so we can settle into the things of God, we can easily take the normal, sensible action everyone else takes. We take no chances and take no leaps. We go about our lives in the same way as everyone else. We can get confused about what we're supposed to be doing, we stop believing in the impossible, and start trying to manipulate our lives to fit neatly into the usual.

Setting the rhythm

Probably all of us have felt those days in our work when we seem to be in tune. We feel steady. Our day seems filled with grace and peace. We flow through the day and through our work, and everything seems to happen with a sense of peace and calm. The melody seems clear. The song flows well. The rhythm is neither too fast nor too slow. It's the way we like our work to go.

But how do we set a pace for the day that takes us through the entire day, regardless of the events that often happen at work? If our goal is to have joy in our work, and to be effective, how do we keep the joy when there are crises and unexpected problems? The easy answer is: "We have quiet time in the mornings." "We pray and the day goes well." Well, sometimes it does.

Many of us struggle with the relationship between our quiet time and our active time. We find we have little time to spend quietly before the day begins. The habit is difficult to set. Even when we begin to take the time, we get interrupted by the phone, the children, the spouse, the needs of the day. Either the ritual stops, or it gets short-circuited, and when we get busy, our active life takes precedence.

Even when we continue, we might have trouble understanding the relationship between our quiet time and our active time and how to use it well. We read the Bible, or spiritual literature, spend some time in meditation or prayer, and then move into the day, hoping a little bit of peace will spill over while we deal with phone calls, meetings, deadlines, impatient co-workers or bosses, employees who don't get their work done, and unexpected crises. And most would agree – it helps. Most would agree – it's important. Many spiritual people begin their day or end their day with these times of contemplation. Without these times, the work doesn't go as smoothly, nor do our lives. These quiet times begin to set a rhythm for the day, with hopes the interruptions won't affect the rhythm established. At the minimum, they usually keep us steady and able to deal better with the frustrations of the active life. But these times can do much more, if we allow them to be more than just a little peace and quiet.

Keeping the rhythm

In most music, there is an ongoing beat that establishes the rhythm of a piece. In a band or orchestra, this might begin with the percussion, but then is also carried through by the deeper instruments – such as the tuba, the bass, the bassoon. The other instruments, such as the flute, the clarinet, the violins, the trumpet, might trill and slide and blare out their melody, but the beat continues, like a heart-beat that keeps the other instruments grounded while still

217

allowing all of the instruments their chance to soar.

If the rhythm is steady and established well, the pace of the music doesn't matter. It can be fast, or it can be slow. Nor does the activity of the melody matter. Nor how many, or how few notes. It is the togetherness and integration of the music that matters, and the way that all the instruments keep the rhythm.

Our quiet time gives us an opportunity to recognize, and commit, to the Ultimate. We get our perspectives straight. We learn how to stay on track, without getting off track with less relevant events, ideas, or commitments. We listen for God's drum.

Yet, there is often a tendency in our work to believe everything is ultimate. We lose the rhythm and get carried away by the activity of the melody and believe it's all about the showy parts.

Those things which seem ultimately important can often be deceptive. Often they seem to be the things which stand out the most – those things which are the loudest, the most dramatic, the most conspicuous. We expect the loudest in any business to get the most business, to get the most awards, to make the most money. But it isn't always true. We feel we have to get the job. We have to close the deal and get the client. We have to finish the report. We have to increase our business. Our business and our work has to be recognized.

But these things get ordered in silence. The pressures and deadlines and the "have tos" take their rightful place during times of quiet and calm and peace. Among the pressures of the day, we can be talked into believing how ultimately important they are. And we certainly work for them. But there is only one ultimate – God. Usually, if we get that straight, other things fall into place.

The unimportant left hand

The importance of the less dramatic and quieter influences can be seen in music. When I was in high school, I had a very fine piano teacher who had taught at Lawrence Conservatory in Appleton, Wisconsin. Before working with Mrs. Byler, I had presumed the most important part of the music would come from my right hand playing the melody. I would practise and practise with my right hand, and when I wanted to get more volume, I would play louder, eventually pounding the piano until the music became rather unpleasant. Mrs. Byler told me it was the left hand that was very important in these sections of music, and that I didn't have to pound with the right hand if I used the left hand to build up the volume and to steady the music. She once told me it would be good for me to only work with my left hand for a while, in order to begin to recognize how much of great music comes from the less-well-known and less-respected left hand. Without setting the rhythm and grounding the music, it won't matter how much activity goes on with the right hand.

The left hand sets the rhythm with what has sometimes been called the "inner voice" of the music. It sets up the many-layered harmony. Although the melody might soar, and pull us in with its inspired high notes, the left hand captures us emotionally with its depth, grounding us like a pulse that matches our heartbeat.

So it is with our work. We put the emphasis on the active life, and on the events we accomplish, and on how well known we are, and sometimes on how showy we can be, not recognizing that it is through the quiet that we tune in to the Ultimate. Often it is our steady inner voice that touches others through our work. Many people might be equally accomplished, and equally achieve great things. But when others think about our work, they often think about that special something we bring to our work that grounds it, that inspires others, that makes it memorable.

Getting in tune

The more demands from our active life, the more important our inner life. The more influential we are in our world, the more dependent we are to keep our perspective through our inner life.

Is it just a matter of perspective? It's more than that. If our inner life isn't in tune, we begin to spread cacophony. Not only do we get out of tune, but everyone around us gets out of tune as well.

For some, like Aneesh Daniel, the quiet time is essential because it is in such sharp contrast to the world he lives in. Aneesh is a Christian film-maker in India. "I live in India, which has very noisy cities. Everyone honks their horns, which is often illegal in other cities." Aneesh's job as a film-maker often includes much frenzy, requiring him to "hurry up and wait!" Aneesh says, "When you're not successful and you're looking for success, you're kneeling down and you're praying. When you are successful, sometimes you don't get a chance to pray, you don't have time to pray and we tend to forget the Lord. Slowly, slowly, the areas which are weaker in us start erupting out. I realize the days when I'm not having my proper devotion I tend to become angry over little things. And then, I realize I did not pray today. Why is this anger coming to me, why am I not able to control it? And because I tend to get angry, it affects other people.

"Morning devotions definitely affect the energy of the day. When you start with prayer, it's the Lord who guides you in the right way. If you planned a meeting at 10 a.m. and then the person calls and cancels, because I prayed in the morning, I know the Lord will take care of it in his own time. I know that the Lord is planting my feet, because it may not be the right time to meet the person because he might not be able to listen because he's tired. That is how the prayer helps – that you leave your day in the Lord's hand and he will take care of it.

"One single incident in the day can diffuse you so much that you can lose all your energy and another incident can boost your energy. Even if something goes wrong after my devotion, I can leave it in the Lord's hand. Often I expect too much to happen. I have worked so hard to get a deal for example, and it does not work, and I say, 'Lord, I prayed and I left it in your hands – do you want this to happen?' So the energy is not your inner energy but it's your relationship with the Lord who governs your day-to-day activities in such a way that it boosts your energy and brings you peace."

Testing our spiritual peace

Often we test whether our quiet time is really affecting our active life in a positive way by how we move through the day. Sometimes I have my own private test which checks out my frustration level when I start the day. This test I call the Hanger Syndrome and it works like this:

Perhaps you're like me – one of the frustrating things in life is the way the hangers in your closet get entangled. In spite of tugging and pulling, they are one of life's smallest, but universal, frustrations. I have a theory that hangers either get into fights during the night, or they are very attracted to each other and fall in love while I sleep. In the morning, in spite of my best efforts, they don't want to leave each other. They're my own little spiritual test. If I can untangle them without being in a hurry, without being frustrated, I figure that my quiet time has set the right tone. If I don't take the peaceful time in the morning, the day seems to start with a minor frustration, which can build. Such a silly thing – but we probably all have those little tiny things in our lives which test our patience, and set a tone for the day.

Offering out

For performers who are very much in the public eye, the time of prayer before a performance becomes important to stay focused.

Christina Baehr is a harpist and singer from Tasmania. She has found that the distractions of performing can easily pull her off her focus, unless she has truly tuned in before she starts playing: "When I write or play music, I move from inward to outward – from something felt in my mind, spirit, muscles, imagination to something that finds existence and purpose in someone else's listening ear. So, instead of 'centering in', I am engaged in 'offering out'. I choose to open my trembling hands and offer to them what I have made. I once premiered a whole program of difficult new music with little time to prepare. One of the composers was so struck by the peace that surrounded me as I played that he asked me afterwards how I'd achieved it. I said simply, 'I pray.' 'You pray?' he repeated, incredulously. His next words came out with intense embarrassment and surprise. 'What – to God?!' My answer meant that I pray before (and sometimes during!) a performance, but thinking back on it, I would now say that my time spent as a pray-er is the foremost thing that equips me to be a player of peacefulness. Playing music, 'offering out' an art that is temperamental, haphazard, and subject to a thousand influences – from the heat of the room to the pattern of the carpet to the dinner you missed to the child in the front row whose legs swing blithely on all the wrong beats – can really unnerve you. Praying and listening to God gives me a reservoir of peace and trust as well as a humbling sense of perspective on my own successes and failures."

Actor Liam Neeson, a Catholic, also thinks of his work as an offering: "I found out that acting could be a form of prayer... I offer my performance as prayer for someone I've worked with as an actor or someone who has died."[96]

For those who are in the midst of war or in the middle of great oppression and suffering, the quiet time is the time of preparation, in order to be able to deal with overwhelming pain. Douglas Millham is dependent on this quiet time to do his work. He says, "Just last month I knelt in tears, holding the burned clothing and other remains of dozens of men, women, and children who had been incinerated in their church in the Rift Valley province of Kenya. As I held the remains of a child's shoe, I wept and shook and cried out to God at the sheer unimaginable weight of this loss and pain. It was just too great to bear. Overwhelmed, the only peace came from surrendering my powerlessness to the God of love I serve. The quiet time / devotion / worship experience is not the place to get away. It is *preparation* for the challenges we face in serving the least and the lost. The moment I encounter the suffering of the world, I am in the absolute center of God's heart. The Apostle Paul wrote: 'I want to know Christ and the power of his resurrection and the fellowship of sharing in his sufferings, becoming like him in his death.'[97] Being one with Christ in his sufferings is the center of the heart of faith, lived out in love to God. How can one be 'off-center' as a Christian when all of your spiritual preparation has finally brought you into his presence? A better question for global inter-cultural servants of God might be this: Does your quiet time take you 'off center' from the heart of God? It's easy to live life inside a spiritual bubble and never experience the passionate and dangerous joy of serving God out on the edge of the Kingdom, out where the water is over your head, where only he can hold you up when the waves crash."

You don't have to play 'The Flight of the Bumblebee'

If we're not centered and tuned in, the work we do becomes frenetic and harried and we take a shotgun approach to what we do. We might feel we need to make twenty calls during the day, and we get into a frenzy, becoming desperate to do them all in hopes some of them yield results. But when we're in tune with our inner life and outer actions, we use economy of movement because we feel guided about what to do, and what not to do. Instead of wasting our activity with doing too much, we rely more on leadings, our intuition, our sense of clarity about what is truly worth doing. We learn to work smarter, rather than working harder. This is not an easy thing to learn and with our flawed desire to either do too much or too little, it's always possible to mishear how we're being led. But we have probably all had the experience of feeling we're told to "wait" before making the phone call, writing the letter, pushing to make something happen. Some call this creative procrastination – recognizing that the waiting can be as important as the doing. And when we're willing to listen, we find out, later, waiting was exactly the right thing to do. We don't need to play too many notes, but just enough for the job at hand.

God's timing is not our timing

People who know music often say that the pauses and the silences between the notes can be as important as the notes themselves. The poet John Milton said, "They also serve who only stand and wait." And sometimes that's exactly what we have to do – simply wait. We need to pause to take the breath, to wait a beat, to have a moment of rest. But waiting can be difficult. We want to do, to act, to make things happen immediately. And everything just seems to take too long. Other times, we're amazed at how much can be done in a short amount of time and how fast we can play while still staying with the rhythm. It's as if time expands and contracts.

Some years ago I was driving a friend to the hospital

for one of her many operations. She knew I was on a deadline for a book and also for several scripts that had to be read for my consulting business. She asked me, "How can you find the time to take me to the hospital, while also doing all of this other work? How are you able to get everything done?"

I answered, "God's time is not regular time. If God wants me to do this for you, then he has to open up extra time for me to get the other things done that I believe he wants me to do. He will simply have to expand time today."

And he did. I got the scripts done over breakfast and made editing notes in the waiting room.

Artists know that creative time can expand and contract. They've had the experience of trying to write a chapter in a book, or work on a painting, or compose music one day and getting nothing done at all, and the next day, their creative muse gets everything done in less time than they could imagine.

People of faith often have the experience of being able to do much in a short amount of time – finish their day's work, do grocery shopping for their neighbor who is ill, help their child with homework, and still take time for some evening devotions.

There's a temptation to believe something has to give in our lives – and we don't have the time to do everything. And sometimes we don't and we're not supposed to. But sometimes we find if we take the time to be faith-full, in prayer and meditation and spiritual reading, there is a smooth transition from our prayer time to our work time and everything gets done in a timely manner. We might feel the pressure to keep busy – always – but many times this is really just filling up our feeling of emptiness. We define ourselves by our accomplishments, by what we got done, which may only lead us to half-baked solutions and lots of extra activity which gets us nowhere. You can't fill up an emptiness of meaning by dumping more activity into it. And often you can't get more done by doing more.

It seems we get the most done and the right things done in our work by tuning in, as much as possible, to God's timing. If we use our own timing, we often do more than necessary. We need more business, so we do twenty more cold calls and thirty more emails. We work late, get stressed, and soon find only a few of those calls are truly effective. But if we take the time to be quiet and still, to take a few deep breaths so this isn't all about being frenzied, we often feel led to what to do and when to do it. We're able to do our work in a more peaceful and more effective way. We listen as much for the "Do this now!" as we do for the "Wait!" We begin to trust more in the natural processes of timing rather than pushing the river to rush a bit faster, which does little good anyway. The river will continue to flow just as it is, with or without our frenzied trying to change things.

There is a saying: when we're not busy, we need to meditate half an hour a day, and when we're really busy, we need an hour. We might, later, try to figure out how we were able to do everything necessary, and it might seem impossible when we count up what was done in the hours we had, but we recognize God's timing often allows us to do far more than we would expect. Our timing works, because we're in tune with God's rhythm.

But God's timing also can work in the opposite way. Rather than getting more done, we're asked to do less.

We often believe that things are supposed to happen fast. We start on a project and think it will take three months, and find that it takes two years. We set out to learn a new skill, thinking that we'll be masters of it within a year or two, and five years later, we're still struggling with all there is to learn. We start a new business, expecting that we'll have a booming business in two or three years, and instead, it takes five or six years. We want success now – right now – but there are some things we don't get until much later.

There is a Jewish saying, "That I should live so long!" It's often said with a sigh, by people who have been waiting and waiting and waiting for their ship to come in, for promises to be fulfilled, and for what was planted to be harvested. And then, just as we wonder if anything will ever come to fruition, suddenly, everything changes and what we planted, blooms. Our work is blessed.

What are we tuning in to?

Although it's often said that we tune into the still and peaceful rhythms at various times during the day, which allows us to cope well with the ups and downs of any job, the Quaker writer, Parker J. Palmer, believes that we tune in to something more – we tune in to what he calls Truth. He doesn't just mean being honest, or ethical, or having integrity as he speaks about this relationship between our contemplative and active life, but that there is something deeper going on during these centering times.

Palmer says that "contemplation and action are not contradictions, but poles of a great paradox that can and must be held together."[98] We find that our active life can get off track because our work, in itself, almost always involves a certain necessity – to earn a living, to get something specific completed. Work has a goal which is external. This can lead to lives of frenzy, exhaustion and even a lack of fulfillment. Palmer says: "In action, we project our spirits outside ourselves. Sometimes we project shadows which do damage to others, and sometimes we project light that others want to extinguish."[99] Contemplation becomes a time when we are changing consciousness in order to have more of an impact on the world around us. We then act, manifesting our inner spirit into the world. "But as we act, we not only express what is in us and help give shape to the world; we also receive what is outside us, and we reshape our inner selves. When we act, the world acts back, and we and the world are co-created."[100] It is an ongoing relationship that changes us and changes the world.

Playing the relationship

The relationship also ripples outward so it's no longer just between our inward center and outward actions, but it begins a dynamic between the people we work with, interact with, even play with.

Irish singer, Brian Houston, describes this back-and-forth of both sides being changed through the music: "I often feel this when I play a show for my hometown crowd and although I've covered this territory many times and they've heard these songs to the point where they know the lyrics inside out; suddenly we find a new way to play this rhythm, this pulse, this joyride of moving dancing melody. In that moment, perhaps due to a mistake or sonic collision a new thing is born and it reveals itself to us and we're no longer the creators but we're being led by the song. Everyone senses it – the audience, the band, the sound engineer, even the cynical promoter raises his head and cocks an eyebrow. Something new is being born right there, in a dingy Belfast bar, and it will never happen quite that way again."

Scotty Vaughn is also a performer. For thirty years, Scotty was one of the Flying W Wranglers – singing cowboys who performed almost nightly in Colorado Springs at the Flying W Ranch Chuckwagon Dinner and Bar-B-Que, as well as throughout the United States – at the Kennedy Center, at Carnegie Hall for the Great American Cowboy Show, as well as in other states. His group was known as one of the foremost cowboy singing groups in the United States. In 2007 Scotty and two other singing cowboys from the Flying W singers, began their own group called "Cowboys for Jesus". Since then, they have sung throughout the United States and in South America. Scotty describes this relationship between his quiet time and his relationship to the audience as dependent upon a sense of brokenness: "When we're broken, God can pour more of himself into us, and that happens when I take the time to be quiet and get centered. I like the concept from Brother Lawrence of practising the presence of God – getting away, feeling the vibes, looking around. I try to get away before we perform, to be quiet, centered, not so much because I'm about to do a spiritual thing, but so I can be broken, so I'm available to him. I wonder who's out there tonight, how can I be used in some way. I pray that I'll be part of God's process through that brokenness, because I realize how much a song can do, and how much God can do through me. If this relationship doesn't happen, it feels hollow and you walk away and think, 'What was that about?' I know that God can even use that, but it's so important to me to be able to sense that. When things don't click in a show those shows feel temporary rather than dealing with the unseen which is eternal. Those shows feel like it's just about what's seen. I know there is an eternal aspect to all of it, but I wasn't present to it. We have a responsibility to the audience but we have a responsibility to God also. In the best shows, suddenly there's a transition and you come at something from a slightly different direction, and a lot of times I'm going from a place I planned to cover to another point I planned to cover, and that's where creativity happens and the Holy Spirit comes in."

In whatever work we do, we are dealing with a variety of relationships. We deal with our relationship to ourselves, our relationship to the work, our relationship to each other, and our relationship to God.

Feeling the true beat

There is another level to this inward and outer work which makes our contemplative time particularly important. Palmer defines is as a time when we "unveil the illusions that masquerade as reality and reveal the reality behind the masks."[101] Our contemplative time allows us to see beyond the "predetermined ends, governed by logic of success and failure... which traps in a system of praise or blame, credit or shade, a system that gives primacy to goals and external evaluations, devalues the gift of self-knowledge and diminishes our capacity to take the risks that may yield growth."[102]

Contemplation is a way to get beyond our egos, beyond the many issues in life that demand that we think of them as ultimate, and to get back to a greater reality. It helps us see beyond the world's expectations and false gods in order to get at what is most important. We become disillusioned and dislocated in order to look at our work from a different, more truthful, standpoint. This has its downside since, as Palmer says, "dislocation is likely to leave us lonely; others do not share our dislocated view of things and sometimes they are threatened by our new truth."[103] But our in-tuneness with the Holy Spirit helps us keep our new-found integrity, and stand against the distortions and cacophony that can be part of our active life.

By becoming clearer about what is truly important, the contributions that we make in our work become more individual and more expressive of who we truly are and what our calling truly is. Palmer says: "An expressive act is one taken because if I did not take it I would be denying my own insight, gift, nature. By taking an expressive act, an act not obsessed with outcomes, I come closer to making the contribution that is mine to make in the scheme of things."[104] We become clearer about our true calling and more able to give through our work.

By taking time to get our priorities straight, we don't spend excessive energy in doing what we think we're supposed to be doing. Instead, we create out of our own inner rhythms, rather than the rhythms of the world which try to shoehorn us into a certain way of being which may not be, at all, what we're called to be.

We can also find the truth by playing what I call the

"What If" game. We ask ourselves to imagine what we'd do if we didn't feel the need for material things and for things of the ego. We might ask ourselves, "What would I do if money were no object?" "What would I do if I removed the world's expectations from this decision?" "What would I do if I only wanted to do the right thing?" This takes away the illusion of importance that we cling to and puts us back into the realm of the Ultimate.

Staying on key

In our work, there is much that can push us off key. Any job has the potential for many negatives that can add dissonance to what we do – from uncooperative co-workers to bosses, clients, and partners who don't understand what we're trying to do. Mark Hanretty and Christina Chitwood are particularly aware of this aspect of their work. They're ice-dancers, skating for Great Britain. In January 2008, they were third in the British Championships and hope to compete in the European Championships, the World Championships, and the Olympics in the future. Mark is from Scotland and Christina is originally from my Quaker Meeting in Colorado Springs.

They find that one of the major pressures comes from the very nature of competition. Mark says, "I like the word 'centered' since there are so many aspects of competition that can get a skater off-center. Often the daily schedule is so intense that staying centered and balanced is a challenge when my day begins at 6 a.m. and ends about 8 p.m. I spend four hours a day practising with Christina and then coach other skaters for the rest of the time. I stay centered by trying to remain true to what is right and good, and by reading positive quotes and other spiritual reading and trying to put my focus on being positive."

Christina likes to pray daily and read something inspirational. "I find meditation helpful for staying centered. If it's a particularly stressful time in my life, I try to say a small prayer and spend some time meditating even if it's only a minute."

One of the elements that can easily get them off-center is the attitudes of others. Mark says: "There's a great deal of competition in ice-skating. Sometimes competition can get cut-throat and cruel. Some people have a dark cloud over them, and even try to use their negative energy to get other skaters off their rhythm. Some athletes are tempted to thrive on the downfall of others. While I can understand this mindset, I believe that is ultimately not beneficial for anyone concerned. I think karmic repercussions will come back to haunt anyone deriving pleasure from the misfortunes of others. As a result, Chrissy and I try to be competitive in the healthiest way. We try to be supportive of other skaters and focus on improving our own performance – knowing that bettering our own standard will lead to the highest echelons we aspire to."

Christina says, "In our skating, it helps that Mark and I are best friends. We try to help each other stay centered. When one of us is having a harder day, we have the attitude of helping each other through. If Mark and I are able to stay centered, then we hope we can touch people's hearts through our skating. We try to stay focused as much as possible on doing what God would want us to do. We focus on skating for God rather than on whether we win or lose. We try not to focus on the placement or outcome of the event but on how we perform and compete ourselves."

They also try to stay centered through the type of music they choose. Mark says, "We like to use positive music. There is a lot of music that sings about negatives in the world and it seems like much of the most popular new music speaks of strife and difficulty – understandable given the depression the news headlines present us with. We personally like Bach, or music like Pachabel's 'Canon in D', or operatic music – music that soars and is inspirational and passionate and makes us want to move."

For all of us, we stay centered through keeping the positive melody in spite of the circumstances.

Playing the tune

God gives us a great deal of freedom in how we play the tune. But God sets the rhythm and if we can stay in step with the rhythm during our day, the various movements of the day will still be grounded. Our individuality is encouraged in our work. There is room for creativity in the work we do and how we do it.

British physicist Wilson Poon thinks of the daily movement we bring to our work as something like a cadenza in music: "In a classical instrumental concerto, there is almost always a section at the end of the first movement named the 'cadenza', where the orchestra goes silent, and the soloist dazzles the audience with his or her technical skills. During the cadenza, the soloist will typically explore a number of different 'keys', sometimes wandering quite far from the key signature of the movement itself. There is only one requirement: that when s/he comes to the point of bringing the whole orchestra back in (marked 'tutti' in the full score), it'd better be in the 'home key'. So, if the movement is in (say) C major, the solo part may quite reasonably be expected to modulate to the dominant (G major) and the relative minor (A minor), or perhaps even C minor. But the solo will always end in C major.

"Nowadays, soloists play pre-composed cadenzas. But in the old days, a composer would often leave the cadenza section of the score blank, inviting the soloist to improvise. Indeed, many cadenzas played today come from great soloists in the past and not the composers of the concertos. Now, there is no such thing as a 'blueprint' for an improvised cadenza – no cadenza can be 'right' or 'wrong'. At the same time, there can undoubtedly be more or less appropriate improvisations (irrespective of the quality of the playing) – those that fit the 'mood' of what has gone before are better, but this is hard to define. In the extreme case, if the soloist dazzles the audience with changing into all kinds of exotic keys, but fails to come back to the home key (C major in the example I mentioned in the previous paragraph), then it is definitely a bad cadenza. Even in this case, however, 'wrong' seems the wrong description of what is going on – 'inappropriate' seems more appropriate!

"The point of saying all of that musical stuff is this: I see each of our work lives as God's challenge to improvise a cadenza. This is consistent with Genesis 1. We can see God as the composer composing the 'concerto of creation', and then bringing on humankind at the end, saying, 'Now over to you!' (More conventionally: 'Be my image; fill and subdue the earth.') In this light, there is no such thing as a 'wrong cadenza'. But there is such a thing as an 'appropriate' cadenza – the biblical word for this is 'wise'. Wisdom comes from conformity with God's will (see, e.g., Psalm 1), now understood in the sense of 'fitting in with the mood of the rest of the concerto.'

"Of course, the Bible offers the important insight that 'sin is real'. So, all of us include inappropriate parts in our improvisations. In the Genesis story, the Tower of Babel can be seen as a brilliantly played cadenza but ending in a funny key – utterly inappropriate, or 'unwise'. But the Bible also tells us that 'redemption is also real, and is more powerful than sin'. Thus, to continue the musical metaphor, even if we somehow land ourselves in C-sharp major at the point of having to dovetail back to the orchestra, the divine conductor can deal with it, and, amazingly, make something beautiful out of it. This is, of course, not a license to sin (i.e., knowingly play inappropriate cadenzas!); rather, it occasions humble thanksgiving."

The cadenza, and the melody, can then take many forms if it always stays with the form that has been set by the composer, and always returns to center. And the type of music needed in our daily active lives will be quite different from one person to another, from one job to another. We become expressive of God's Spirit. Christina Baehr says: "When we do our best, our skill is exerted unconditionally moving from the inner, then upward and outward, offering out, throwing energy into others in the most vulnerable and generous way."

Questions for reflection and discussion

1. What spiritual disciplines do you do to set the rhythm of your work?
2. How do you see the relationship between the contemplative life and the active life? Which one is more natural to you?
3. What are the problems you encounter keeping the rhythm you set in your quiet time? What kinds of things get you off rhythm? Under what circumstances do you encounter the Hanger Syndrome, or other problems that get you off rhythm?
4. Do you ever "offer out"? When?
5. Discuss your cadenzas in life, when you feel you are improvising and finding freedom in your work.

Scripture to consider

Read some of the verses about music and song: Judges 5:3; 1 Chronicles 6:32; 25:7; Psalms 27:6; 45:8; 57:7; 92:1; 98:4; 108:1; Ephesians 5:19; Exodus 15:1; Psalms 40:3; 96:1.

Part 3

Nearing and Arriving at the Goal

CHAPTER 9

Save Time for Tragedy, Save Room for Miracles

It makes all the difference whether one sees darkness through the light or brightness through the shadows.

David Lindsay

Success in our work gives us riches of many kinds. We have the money for what we need when we need it. We have the clout to be influential – and to give expression to our own values, wishes, and goals. Although our success makes demands on us, we usually have some independence and some control over our lives, if we choose to take it. True, there can be more pressures and stresses, but the Bill Gateses of the world can decide whether to say "yes" or "no" to invitations and can delegate to others. For many others, there's little choice.

There can be an embarrassment of riches for those who have the opportunity to choose whether to say "yes" to the conference in Maui, the seminar in Paris, the meeting in Rome or whether to accept the speaking engagement in Buenos Aires, Moscow, Tokyo, or Sydney. Perhaps, instead, the person will choose to have a little retreat in their 20,000-square-foot home in the mountains or by the sea. It is not a sad story when one of these people says, "I'm so stressed trying to decide between all these choices!"

Although those who have reached their goals have many opportunities, and can decide which ones to take, for those on the road to success, striving to reach a goal, there can be all the demands to say "yes" to anything and everything that could get them ahead. They become overbooked with commitments, hoping to get their name out there, hoping the powers-that-be will notice.

But just as the Incredibly Successful People and the People On Their Way Up have blocked out their schedule neatly and to their utmost satisfaction, tragedy can strike.

Probably everyone reading this book has had some tragedy in their lives – something which forced them to stop everything and to respond to the unwanted interruption just when things seemed to be going well. It might have been the moment when the woman discovered a lump in her breast, and realized that for the next months, or even years, life would not be the same. Or the man who finally found a day to get out and ride his Harley and had an accident that laid him up for months of operations and recuperation and rehabilitation. Or a person who was caught up in a natural disaster – a tornado that destroyed the home, an earthquake that demanded expensive repairs, a hurricane that swept away a household of fond memories and special things. For the next few years, the response to the tragedy will interrupt everything in their lives and demand constant attention.

Or the tragedy may happen to someone near to you. A mother is nearing death and needs your presence at her side. Your father can no longer live on his own and needs a week of your life to help him move. Your friend has just lost her husband and needs hours of your time to help her grieve.

Some of us will have tragedies come to us, personally, and others will have to make choices about how to respond to the tragedies of others. All will demand a response.

A tragedy, like the sins mentioned in the earlier chapter, can be big or small, important or seemingly trivial, but these moments change our lives. They jolt us awake and force us to do something about the problem. The way we respond to tragedy tells us much about our value system, our spiritual choices, and our spiritual priorities.

Responding, not ignoring

For the spiritual person, this moment of decision is an important step on the road to success. If we feel that we've been called or led to our work, and recognize that our work is doing good in the world, any interruption seems like a detour and even a spiritual test. Is this person, whether ourselves or others, more important than the work that we're doing? Should we just struggle through, the best we can, because we believe that the continuation of our job is of ultimate importance? And it raises spiritual questions: Why did God allow this to happen? If I'm doing God's work, why would God want this good work to be interrupted? How can I continue to do what I'm called to do, and also recognize that part of my spiritual life is my compassion and love for others?

There are plenty of people, even spiritual people, who don't choose to respond. They have an illness, but they muddle through, ignoring the physical warnings, limping to work in spite of their pain, skipping doctor's appointments, determined to beat it by continuing as if nothing is wrong. Their friend or relative needs their help, but they can only spare an hour. Yet who has really lost out by this lack of response?

I lived in Los Angeles during the Northridge earthquake in 1994. Although the damage to our home was minimal (about $2000 worth), we had a week of thousands of aftershocks. My friend and her son were without electricity so they moved into our home for two days as we ate the frozen food from her refrigerator and ours. But in spite of the disruption, I was determined to continue with my consulting work. I read scripts through the aftershocks, even though my concentration was disrupted. I typed out long reports, even though I knew my focus was off. In retrospect, I think I was wrong about this. I don't remember anything about the work I did that week. But I do remember how our neighbors all checked up on each other, going out at 4:30 a.m. with flashlights to make sure everyone was all right. I remember how comforting it was to sit with my husband, my friend, and her son, through the many aftershocks. I remember trying to figure out how to comfort our pets – two California land tortoises – since it was clear they were stressed by the bumpy ride. I remember the party a friend gave a few days later, for us to celebrate that we were all OK and to share our experiences. I remember the calls to friends to make sure everyone was all right and our shared efforts to clean up. That was what the week was about – responding to the earthquake, not trying to continue as if nothing had happened.

There is something good that can come out of tragedy – whether it's our awakening to a problem we ignored, or a greater sense of community, or an opportunity to rethink and deepen ourselves. We may return to our work in much the same way after some time has passed, or it may be a new road that opens up for us. In many cases, it reminds us whose agenda we're supposed to be following.

The flip-side of tragedy

British physicist Dr. Wilson Poon asks the key question we all need to ask ourselves when tragedy comes to us: "Any old fool can praise God looking at a beautiful sunset. But what about speaking of God in a tsunami? In the bacterium that causes the Black Death? The same dust cloud that gives an extra-beautiful sunset causes respiratory diseases further eastwards. The writer from the Middle Ages, Denys the Areopagite,[105] challenges us to speak of God even from those parts of creation that repel us. He says that if all of creation is created by God, then we must learn to speak of God from *all* of creation. Only after we have done that do we realize that all language is inadequate, and are then reduced to silence."[106]

The Book of Job speaks about this same process of looking for the meaning when bad things happen to us. Job tried to figure it out intellectually, asking all his friends the "Why?" questions. God let Job know that the answers do not lie with the "Why?" but with the recognition of God's presence and power beneath all the whys. And Job was reduced to silence in the midst of answers far beyond anyone's logic.

Wilson Poon continues: "Science has a key function here – it directs our attention to all kinds of things, including the tsunami and Plague bacterium. The scientists who study these things can sense the power, the intricate beauty, etc. – they are in the best position to speak of God starting from these parts of creation." Poon adds: "To paraphrase Denys, I think the most important thing science teaches us is about the humility of God. God appears content to create a universe in which the presence of Godself is unobvious, to say the least. Scientists really can, and must, carry on their work without recourse to divine intervention." Although miracles do happen in the midst of tragedy, there are times that other qualities come to the forefront.

Tragedy can polish us

Dr. Ted Baehr produces 420 *Movieguide®* radio and television programs per year, teaches, speaks, writes books, and publishes *Movieguide* magazine. He grew up in the entertainment industry as the son of two early Hollywood stars and has a PHD in theology and a JD from NYU School of Law. He clearly has important work to do, for which he has been well prepared.

But since the mid 1990s, his wife Lili has had cicatricial pemphigoid – a disease that attacks the mucous lining of her eyes and body. It's a painful disease that has destroyed one of her eyes, damaged her mouth, produced boils, and could lead to death. And it affects the entire family as they all learn to cope with the illness.

Ted uses the metaphor of a rock polisher to explain how tragedy can actually help our spiritual development: "A minister friend of mine was counseling a couple in Washington at their home. The husband had MS so they had suffered economic tragedy and he had lost his job as a result. As he was counseling them, there was this awful grinding noise in the background – their son's rock polisher. If you have children or have ever been to Toys-R-Us, you will know that a rock polisher looks like a little vertical cement mixer with a funnel, a belly and three gears at the bottom. You throw the rocks that you find at the pond or stream into the machine. If they're precious or semi-precious, they'll polish, and if they're not, they'll be ground to bits. The minister asked if the parents could turn it off. When they said that the polishing takes months and the machine had to be left running, the minister asked, 'How do they polish?' The husband explained, 'All the gears do is throw the rocks up in the air and the rocks polish by hitting up against each other.' And he said, 'How long does it take?' 'The more precious they are, the longer they take to polish.' 'Well, how do you know when it's finished?' 'When you can take the stone out of the rock pile and see your face in it.'

"The minister used the rock polisher to help the family. He said they were like the stones. The loss of the husband's job was battering them up against each other. If they were precious they would polish. God would know when they were polished when He could see His face and likeness in them."

Ted continued: "Every human being is a little solar system – they want to be their own lord and savior and to control their own life. But we don't control much of our life and even when we think we're controlling it, we're not. One way we try to do that is to get away from people, but actually God's system is that our relationships and our situations polish each of us. The church, the family, our jobs, for instance, are our rock polishers. The circumstances of sickness, disease, poverty are really just the gears that throw us up in the air and force us to hit up against each other. If we abandon each other, if we abandon people, if we abandon coming together, we don't get polished. We get polished by knocking off the rough edges of each other. So we need each other to polish each other."

The tragedies that we don't want may actually create in us a person who can better show the face of God through our work and our lives.

Some reasons for tragedy

Ted continues the metaphor: "That said, now we get to the gears. The Bible says there are four reasons that bad things happen to people: the world, the flesh, the devil, and discipline.

"Number one is the world. We live in a world that has laws designed into it. If a tsunami or earthquake comes and destroys a business or hurts someone, it's not because it's a particular personal attack. It's because it's part of the world. Most of the problems come because we live in the world. That's what happens when these God-ordained natural laws come together in time and place. If a bus driver skids on the road because of ice, it's not his fault or the ice's fault or God's fault. It's just how Creation operates.

"Number two is the flesh. For a lot of people the flesh is what takes them out because they're constantly giving in to the flesh. Mayors, politicians, and businesspeople are often in the news because they succumbed to greed, lust, gluttony, or other temptations of the flesh. Enron and John Edwards are good examples.

"The third is the devil – someone actively attacking you through slander, envy, malice, greed, or something else. The Greek word for slander is *diablos* – the accuser, an attack that devastates us.

"And the fourth is God directly working on us. That happens with a few people who are usually called saints, although everybody in the body of God is a saint. I tell the story of David Livingstone who went to Africa, thinking he was going to convert all of Africa, stop the slave trade and heal the sick. He goes to Africa and he converts one Chief, who later recants. Livingstone loses his children to sickness and ends up being nursed by slave traders. So the most scandalous newspaper in the USA sends H.M. Stanley, a wicked reporter, over to Africa to find and expose Livingstone. He finds him after a year in the very little town of Ufifi, being taken care of by the slave traders and Livingstone has turned into this kind loving person in whom one could see the face of God. And Stanley says, 'I came to expose what a fraud you were,' and Livingstone says, 'You're right. I haven't achieved any of my goals.' And Stanley was so impressed with Livingstone's humility that he came to Christ. As a result, he then wrote his famous book entitled *Through Darkest Africa* which was read by the King of Belgium, the last slave-trading European country. The king was influenced by Stanley and became the last European ruler to stop the slave trade. Also, as a result of Stanley's book, Revival broke out in Central Africa that continues today. The moral of the story is: Livingstone lost his wife and his children and didn't get the goal he expected to get, but through all this, God was more concerned with Livingstone's character and attitudes than his accomplishments. Circumstances polished Livingstone into a precious jewel who witnessed in word and deed to the love of God."

Although the lessons of this story are many, it may tell us that we don't know how we'll accomplish our goals, and that detours and sidetracks may be the way that God works through us so we can have far more influence than we had ever hoped.

Recognizing the blessings of tragedy

The challenges of a tragedy are many. Ted explains: "A couple of years ago when Lili almost died because they put her through the wrong chemotherapy, I went through a period of being angry at God. And a Christian leader said to me, 'Oh, you can't be angry at God.' So I spent about two months feeling guilty about being angry at God. Then I realized that God was bigger than my anger since Jeremiah and Job and the other giants of the Bible had, at one time or another, been angry at God.

"Then in confirmation of the blessing in the midst of the trials, my third son came up to me and said, 'Dad, many of the kids are on drugs and into sex and are lost and some have never recovered.' But he continued, 'The reason we're not is because we've had to learn how to have compassion because of the fact we have had to take care of Mom, driving her and doing things for her.' That doesn't take away the pain of having lost her eye and the pain of the boils, but the good part of it, if there's any good, is that God uses these things to bring us to be more compassionate, more loving, more gracious.

"And the affliction we receive gives us the ability to then comfort others who are afflicted. And our job in life is not just making widgets and gadgets, and as the Bible says there's no end to the writing of books, but the most important thing we can do as we are thrown together is to allow others to knock off our impurities so we can learn to be compassionate, to have empathy with others, to have a deepening of wisdom, to bring joy to others – to have the image of God. So I don't see this as being a sidetrack, I see this as being the main track. I see the sidetrack as trying to keep up with our email. I see the sidetrack as getting so solipsistic that we forget there are higher responsibilities.

"The truth is, we're not made to live forever, we're made to wear out like the Velveteen Rabbit who got tattered from being loved to death. It's not a question of going to die, it's about what we do on that road as we lose our hair.

"Through these tragedies, if we allow ourselves to be polished by them, we learn to give. Giving is really love – you touch someone's heart, and the more you give, the more joy you have."

Learning about ultimates

Tragedies have the potential to deepen and broaden us, in order to make us more able to do God's work. They have the potential to transform us and redeem us, in the midst of suffering and despair.

In our usual work-a-day lives, our work calls forth certain qualities from us that we need to do our jobs. In my work as a script consultant, I need to be creative and analytical. It's not a requirement that I be compassionate. I need to be nurturing and encouraging, but I can still do my job well without being empathetic. I need to be responsible and in control, but I don't need to let the mysteries of life take over. I need to be good at time management, but it's not essential that I'm patient.

But when any tragedy strikes, those qualities that are underdeveloped within me must come to the forefront. When my mother was declining and nearing death, I had to spend many days simply sitting by her bedside doing very little. My goals were now unimportant. I learned something about patience, which I could later bring to my own work when solutions didn't present themselves quickly to me to solve a problem.

When my sister was dying of ALS, I learned about what it means to surrender to the mystery of life. Toward the end of her life, I asked if she had any intuition about when she would die. By that time, she was unable to talk, so she simply wrote, "God's timing!" She taught me a valuable lesson about surrender, and about recognizing how much in life simply is beyond our control.

And she taught me about compassion and empathy, about grace and acceptance, simply by how she dealt with her own illness. This doesn't mean that I've learned these lessons as well as those I've been practising every day in my work, but it does mean that I've been expanded and deepened as a person, and have more resources to give to my clients and students.

Tragedy has the potential to add something to our character, to complete us, to polish us so we can better show the image of God.

This deepening connects us with the ultimates of life – with death, with the meaning of illness and suffering, with the love and even joy that can come from the depths of life. When responding to tragedy, it's difficult to remain on the superficial layer of life. We are rooted in the depth of life, and there we can find new meanings and deeper understandings and a clearer perspective which, in turn, enhances what we bring to our work.

Using the tragedy

Sometimes the tragedy is so great and unexpected that it seems impossible that anything good can come out of it. Sometimes the tragedy is not just the ordinary wearing down that comes as people near the end of their lives, or become sick from physical problems that affect so many people. There are times when true evil causes a tragedy and it's unclear how God can ever turn this into good.

Craig Scott was sixteen and a student at Littleton High School near Denver, Colorado when two students went on a rampage in his high school, first killing his sister, Rachel, and then twelve other students and teachers, including his two best friends who were with him in the library. The shooting was not only a shock, and a tragedy, but it led to copycat threats and other school shootings, shattered families, and shocked a nation. Craig eventually learned to see the hand of God in this experience and in his life, not because God caused it, but because God was able to make something out of it.

He looks at this experience through a prophetic perspective: "When I was born my Dad knew one guy who had, he believed, the gift of prophecy and he trusted him. This man said a prophetic word over me that one day I would be a leader of leaders. My parents told me about this when I was twelve years old. My Dad would tell me the story about David in the Bible, and how he had to go through these hard things before he would become king. My Dad also told me this great story called *Home in the King's Chariot*. It talked about horses that could be free and wild, but those horses could never pull the king's chariot because the horses that pulled the king's chariot had to go through discipline and hard times and being instructed. It was a great honor to do this. So I had this belief even when I was young that for anybody to do anything great in this world they would probably have to go through hardship."

During the Columbine shooting, Craig was in the library where a number of people had been killed and wounded. Craig says, "I was in the library underneath the table with my two friends who had been shot and killed. I didn't know where the shooters had gone. I was completely paralyzed with fear and I couldn't move or think clearly and my body was totally numb, and the only thing I could do was pray and the only thing I asked God for was to take away the fear. I was experiencing so much fear I can't describe it, I thought my heart was going to stop beating. But the moment I prayed, I felt relieved, I felt I was able to move, and I heard God speak to me – usually God speaks to me through the Spirit and guides me through choices and feelings – but that time I thought I heard something say to me, 'Get out of there', so I was the first student in the library to stand up and I yelled at everyone else, 'Let's get out of here, they're gone!' I helped a girl who had her shoulder blown off and she was rocking back and forth for help, and we ran out of the emergency exit. As soon as we got out and got behind the police car, the two shooters came back to the library. They had done all the shooting and came back. My belief is that God saved my life. At the same time I believe he took Rachel's life in his hands. The anointing was for me to go on and carry on."

Even though Craig was only a sophomore in high school, he saw that this experience was preparing him and deepening him.

When the shooting occurred, Craig didn't have a specific plan for his life, although he expected to go to college and maybe go into psychology. Craig says: "Columbine has contributed to many things that have happened to my life since then. But it wasn't as if I had a plan that got ruined, since I didn't have a plan. But I came up with a plan afterwards."

The tragedy led Craig to a different kind of work than he would ever have expected. The new plan came out of his response to the tragedy. "My first interview was two days after Columbine on April 22 with Katie Couric. I was very raw, and my Dad said that while he was watching the interview, he felt there was an anointing."

Shortly after Craig's first interview, his father, a former minister, began speaking about the tragedy and the lessons to be gained from this. Craig says, "I began to do more interviews, then started traveling with my Dad to speaking events where I usually spoke for five or ten minutes. At this time there were a number of people who had gone through the tragedy who wanted to move on and didn't feel the need to talk about it, but I was talking about it because I felt like it was doing something for the audience."

Craig felt that he had to embrace the experience in some way, in order to find the meaning in it, rather than move away from the experience. He says, "There's a difference between holding on to something that's negative and dwelling on something that's negative, but pain is not always negative. Pain can be a purifying thing."

Dodging the cross

Australian theologian Dr. Desmond Ford of the Seventh Day Adventist Church puts this idea into theological terms. He says if we don't face the experience, we are "dodging the cross". He says, "While on the cross with pain we will often be tempted to take a short cut. We need to be careful at that point."[107] Ford instead advises that we see the positive aspects of suffering and tragedy. "Whatever reminds us of the fragility of life and our dependence upon God is to some extent salutary. Whatever prevents us from building our nest securely down here below in such a way as to forget our Creator, is a disguised blessing, to some degree at least."[108]

How we confront tragedy can be quite individual and means discernment in our way of responding. Having to find our way through the pain has the potential to lead us to wisdom. Craig recognized that there is a fine balance between not talking, and talking too much. "I think in the long run it's more healthy for the person that chooses to talk about it and to be willing to be open about it instead of closing in on it. More healthy because there's a release when you do talk about it and it helps a person in the long run to move on. But there were times I talked about it too much and it was unhealthy for me because it was holding me. I was starting to have the same conversations with people. I would go on autopilot when I'd be talking with people."

How does one become authentic through this

process? Craig says that he had to learn to go off autopilot. "I had to learn to say something different or to think about something in a different way, or to focus my attention on someone else – to try to be in the moment."

Changing directions

For Craig, the tragedy also changed the direction of his life and his work. Craig became an international speaker on the tragedy, a speech which became the number-one high school program in the United States. While continuing to speak about the lessons of compassion that can be learned from the tragedy, he became interested in film-making. Craig says, "I got interested in film-making after the shooting because the television show, *Dateline*, decided to follow me for a year and they did this story called 'The Long Journey Back'. They gave me a camera and asked if I would film my life so I carried this camera around for a year. I took all the footage and edited the tapes with the help of a friend. I then went to Colorado Film School, then worked on a movie as the assistant to the producer and as a stunt double. I realized how much of an impact a film can have, especially since the two shooters had been influenced negatively by the film *Natural Born Killers* which they watched about a hundred times."

Craig's goals changed as a result of the shooting. He is now writing, directing and producing short films, and is scheduled to be a producer on a film about his sister's life. "I want to do stories that inspire and ennoble people and that eventually lead audiences to make better choices with their lives. It's a lofty goal, but I know there are films that I've watched that made me want to be a better person. I do believe that I can figure out ways to use film in storytelling as a way to teach, to inspire, to challenge, to help people think."

Deepening through tragedy

What are the good things that come out of a tragedy? Like the California earthquake, or the illness of Lilly Baehr, Craig learned that tragedy can deepen us. "After tragedies people put differences aside and come together, and a lot of times people become more sensitive to one another and say the things that are very meaningful to one another. I saw that after Columbine our community did that, and people became very sensitive to life and death. After Columbine, if somebody said to me, 'I'm really depressed and I'm having thoughts of suicide' that would really affect me and I would stop everything to be there for that person. I think that when people go through tragedy they can become more compassionate. It deepens you, deepens your conversations with people. Since Columbine, I have had a lot more serious and authentic conversations because somebody would find out what I went through and they'd ask questions and they'd open up to me about something serious they'd gone through. If I was on a airplane, perhaps talking to a total stranger, instead of talking about the weather or some vacation spot, we'd talk about someone they lost in their lives and how that affected them. I felt that was a privilege. There were probably other people in their life that they've been around for years that they haven't told this stuff to. So I felt that it was a position I needed to handle with care, and that I needed to be thankful for – to realize it was an honor and a privilege to be in that position."

But where is God in the midst of this? Craig believes God was always present. "I saw God's hands behind it all, composing a bittersweet symphony. Not that he caused that day, but behind that day, behind everything, and behind the tragedy, he was still in control. He was composing this beautiful bittersweet symphony and that he had a plan and purpose behind it all. I think about when Christ was crucified and I think about what that day must have been like and what an evil and wrong and bloody and unfair and unjust tragedy it was, but behind it all, God's hand was at work."

Craig continues: "My Dad had a similar experience. When he heard that the shooting had happened and he left work and was driving to the school, he kept hearing the same words repeated over and over again – 'A spiritual event! This is a spiritual event!'

"Tragedies put priorities in place – relationships and people and even God became top priority. It pushes people to search for deeper answers and truth and to push them to find out who they are. I think finding out who you are is ultimately finding out who you are in God because God created you, so who better to tell you who you are than your creator? You learn to move with the tragedy."

Make room for miracles

Just as tragedy can change the direction of our lives, so can miracles. Just as tragedy demands that we take the time to turn away from the road we're on, to respond to the road we're asked to travel on, miracles also demand that we recognize them and allow them in our lives. They can easily be bypassed, or even go unnoticed.

For most of us, our work lives are filled with daily miracles, although we often don't see them as such. But sometimes we do see an ordinary event as miraculous because it happened at just the time that we needed it.

Martha Williamson knows about miracles and about angelic interventions, since she's been writing about it for years. She was the executive producer and head writer of the television show, *Touched by an Angel*, which can be seen in over 100 countries around the world. Martha defines miracles in a number of ways. She says, "Most episodes of *Touched by an Angel* were about people making spiritual choices which could be considered miracles because they were supernatural. There was one episode about a healing that was really about an act of forgiveness which made room for healing to happen. But many miracles happen because we're in the right place at the right time. And we happened to be in the right place at the right time because we responded to the nudging that got us there. Just as we may be called to a particular job and we choose to follow that call, we are called almost daily to do one thing rather than another, to go right rather than left, to make a phone call or go to a meeting, even though we hadn't planned to do it that day. This means being open to God's nudging and taking advantage of what is put before us, even if it's not what we asked for. I think I have seen more miracles in my life because I finally felt I had that bubble of success around me that gave me the courage and chutzpah to boldly go to the Throne and not be so concerned about what others thought. And I've been willing to make choices that haven't always made sense to me, as I've learned to trust that it's often God leading me in ways that have become naturally supernatural."

For nine years, Martha wrote and produced the long-running *Touched by an Angel*. She sees that the synchronicity that brought her to that opportunity can be traced to a string of circumstances that led her there. "I think there is a progression of miracles that occur in our lives that we may, or may not, recognize. I can go back to before I was born and think of the guy in the Revolutionary War that dodged a bullet and because of that, I ended up being born 200 years later. In my own life, I can think of one moment after another when, if I had turned left instead of right, my whole life would have been different.

"As I was growing up, my best friend was Mary Ann. Her father had moved from Oklahoma to Colorado when I was eight years old and they moved right behind us. We became best friends. When we were seventeen, she wanted to be a pompom girl and needed my vote to become one, but I couldn't vote for her unless I was a member of the Pep Club. I joined the Pep Club to help my friend who had moved here ten years ago. On the night I voted another friend that was there that night said I should meet the Admissions Counselor at Williams College. The admissions counselor said, 'If you apply, I will accept you.' So, I went to Williams College instead of Colorado College where I had intended to go. Almost four years later, I'm hungry and I walk into a snack bar, and some guy is sitting there that I know from the theater, and he says, 'I'm supposed to be the host for some Alumni-in-the-Entertainment-Industry event, but I have to study so would you take over for me?' As a result of that, I end up meeting the guy who got me my first job in show business. So there are these little miracles, this synchronicity, that we may not recognize."

Martha sees this synchronicity occur throughout her professional life, but realizes that she needs to be open to God. "Let me give you two examples," she says. "The most regular arrival of miracles came once a week when I was writing *Touched by an Angel*. I wrote or rewrote every episode of that show for nine years, 213 total. Then for three of those nine years I produced *Promised Land* simultaneously. I'd call it a miracle that I could write things so quickly. I'd sit there and look at the computer with my hands on the keys and just said, 'OK, Lord, now what?' You can't just keep cranking out and cranking out and stay inspired. Writing for these shows is different from, perhaps, a show like *Law and Order* which is more procedural. For these shows, you have to dig deep into your heart and pull it out, and make that certain layer to inspire, yes, also entertain and hopefully inform, but definitely inspire. Before the show is over, people want to feel something, they want whatever they're watching to tap into themselves emotionally."

Like Martha, we may have, at times, found that there's a flow to our work that we might find incomprehensible. Why should we be able to get so much done in so little time? Where did that idea come from? How did everything happen so smoothly? How did we manage to meet just the person we needed, at the time we needed him?

Martha believes we have to pray about the opportunities offered to us and to not be overly concerned when our schedule is disrupted. Perhaps it's disrupted to make room for a miracle. Martha says, "I was trying to finish my first two-hour movie for television, which was about human rights in China. I had seven days to write a two-hour movie, which is ridiculous, and on top of that, I had been invited to Denver many weeks before and I had made a commitment to go there and give a speech, and I couldn't cancel on them. So I'm stuck. I didn't know how to make this story work, and I knew I couldn't just make something up since this was based on real events and real situations and based on people's lives. If you get this wrong, I'm sending out the wrong information to people who could make a difference – a good difference or a very dangerous one. So, I go to Denver to do the speech. After the speech, all I want to do now is to get back home. But for some reason I missed the flight. I've never missed a flight in my life. We get booked on a later flight, and while waiting, I look up, and see the Panda Express on the second floor, so I decide to go up and get something to eat. Why did I choose Panda Express instead of the Mexican food? I don't know. But as I eat, I notice a Chinese man sitting next to us talking to a woman, and what are they talking about? Human rights in China. I'm bold, and tell him that 'I must apologize for interrupting your conversation but I don't think it's an accident that we're sitting next to each other.' I end up pitching the entire story and showing him the hole in my story, and he tells me the way to fix it. I ended up finishing the story on the way home. If I hadn't missed the plane, if I hadn't seen the Panda Express, and if I hadn't sat at that table – I would have continued to struggle. This has happened so many times to me in my work – being led to the right person at the right time, to the right information just when I need it.

"It's not about the watchmaker God who puts it down and walks away. It's not a marionette God. We have a deeply involved God who has created through daily opportunities and miracles such a mysterious intricacy in our lives." Martha uses the same image as Craig – that God is a conductor. We need to tune in so the flow and the music begins to happen through us.

Many miracles are a matter of timing. We either get with the rhythm and it moves us, or we decide we'll do it our way, so we're not where the flow is happening. And as a result, the flow isn't happening through us either. Martha says, "The closer we get to a relationship with God, the more in sync we are, the timing is usually going to work for us. And we're more likely to be in the place where the miracle will occur. Instead of fighting the surprises and the changes in our plan, sometimes we need to just go with the flow. We get in tune with the movement and allow the miracle to happen without resisting it. It's about showing up. I think this can frighten a lot of people, because we're allowing God to be in control."

Martha sees ways that we shut the door on miracles: "Sometimes the folks who are so successful financially may actually lose touch with the people who made us successful. If you are in the airport and you're a regular person and you miss your flight, you might end up getting exactly what you need because you had to stop off at the Panda Express and meet the one person who can set you off on a better course. But the more successful someone gets, the easier it is for someone to hire the private plane, snap their fingers and bypass the line and go into the private waiting room, and have someone bring you your coffee. I've done both and discovered that being expedient may make things easier, but you can also miss a lot of down-to-earth miracles along the way."

There is, beneath the tragedy and beneath the miracle, a blessing that can be found if we don't bypass it, if we don't ignore it, if we learn to recognize it. As a result, we come back to our work with greater spiritual riches and sometimes, like Job, also with greater material riches. We often become more in tune with the people we work with. We often find that the time we seem to have lost, actually seems to be found as we suddenly seem to accomplish more than expected. We haven't taken a detour at all. This was all used as part of a greater plan.

Questions for reflection and discussion

1. Has your work ever been interrupted by tragedy? What happened?
2. How did you decide what to do to balance the calling to your work and the calling to help yourself or others?
3. Were you able to see God's hand during the tragedy or during the miracle? Were you able to see God's hand in retrospect?
4. Would you define a miracle in the same way that Martha defines it? Are there some other characteristics you might emphasize as you think about the miracles in your own lives?
5. How did the tragedy or the miracle deepen you? Did it turn you in new directions? Did it help you become better at your work?

Scripture to consider

Read the stories of people who encountered great tragedies and turns in the direction of their lives. These would include the story of Joseph in slavery and prison, exiled from his family (Genesis 37–45), the story of Moses (Exodus 2–24), the Book of Job. Even Cain is said to have had the hand of God protecting him (Genesis 4:15). How do you see God's hands conducting?

Chapter 10

Becoming Unimportant

He must become greater, I must become less.

John the Baptist (John 3)

Some years ago I was on a one-week horseback-riding vacation in Spain. One of the riders had recently retired as a headmaster at an exclusive private school in the eastern United States. He said during his tenure money was raised, new buildings were built, academic scores went up – by every indication, he had been highly successful at his job. When he announced his retirement, the Board asked what it would take for him to stay longer. They promised him a higher salary, a renovated house, more benefits. But ultimately, he decided to retire. I asked him why. He said, "Because I wanted to become unimportant again."

As we rode along by the beautiful haciendas and vineyards of southern Spain, I realized that I had chosen to return to horseback riding in my forties for exactly that same reason, even though less consciously. I was doing well in my business, loved the work I did, was able to deal with almost all problems that I encountered, and felt that I had achieved a good level of mastery in my work. To balance my life, I wanted to become a learner again, to be vulnerable in the way we all are when we're first learning something new. Although I had no desire to stop doing the work I loved, I wanted to add another element to my life and I felt there was something intrinsically spiritual about this desire, although I couldn't define what it was. Perhaps it was the desire to experience a First Joy again – that sense of passion and happiness that we often feel when we begin our work, and feel hopeful and expectant about possibilities, and feel that we've found our heart's desire.

I noticed that many of my colleagues who had achieved success in their work also were turning to leisure activities that were quite different from their daily work. They were excited about this new journey, and accepted, with great humor, their stumbling efforts at learning something new. Usually they chose to enter into an activity where they would no longer be the top of the heap, but would become the unimportant novice, with little ability and little knowledge.

Some chose to balance their lives by deliberately choosing a hobby or leisure-time activity that was outside their usual comfort zone. The people who had devoted their lives to mental activity took up golf, tango lessons, and tennis. The person who had a highly active physical life learned a foreign language, joined a Great Books Club, or started playing an instrument.

Among the many reasons they all turned to something new, it seemed they recognized the dangers of pride and ego and desired to expand their sense of joy.

Keeping the ego in check

Why is this process of becoming unimportant, in one form or another, important?

We begin any new work as beginners, with some hopes of becoming good at what we do. In many jobs, our success depends on achieving mastery in our work.

The professional tennis player achieves mastery over strategy, the spin, the lob, and being able to put the ball exactly where she or he desires. When mastery is achieved, there are accolades, rewards, more money, and more sources of income as they sign lucrative deals for ads and sports announcing.

The surgeon becomes an expert at a specific type of surgery and sees patients being healed and the work being recognized. The teacher notices that the students learn better and succeed because the teacher knows how to present material and how to make learning fun.

Rewards and adulation don't always come with mastery. There are plenty of people who do well at their jobs, but the jobs may not be high-profile ones which give extra recognition for their work. These jobs have to be their own reward because no outside power will come along to add extra money, or extra gratitude, to the work.

But for those who are in positions where mastery leads to acclaim, it's easy to believe that one has become the Best There Is, the King of the Mountain, the Queen Bee in the larger world of worker bees. The ego can easily get out of control, believing one's own press and crowing about one's own specialness.

Of course, sometimes the ego uses hyperbole and one isn't quite as special as he, or she, might think. I've been in more than one seminar given by an egocentric colleague who informs me, "Everyone in my class came up to tell me that this was the best class they had ever taken!" Since I had been there, I was aware that out of the 150 people who had been in the class, there were about 25 crowded around the teacher at the end of the class. And, of course, my colleague had not heard the comments in the hallway during the breaks when students said, "A really great class, but what an ego!"

Sometimes the class was great, but the extra crowing diminished it, rather than enhancing it. Instead of the teacher helping the student increase, the teacher puffed up and made himself, or herself, the center of attention. The whole point of mastery – to be able to help others become masters – is then lost. One teacher once told me, "We don't want to tell them too much, or they'll become better than we are!" I answered, "Isn't that the point? That's how civilization moves forward!"

Some spiritual people decide to put themselves in the position of the student, learning a new skill to become unimportant again. Not only do they gain insights about what the beginners in their own field are going through, but it puts the ego in check since they will, undoubtedly, feel plenty of humiliation. I have, more than once, quoted a favorite line of dialogue from the James Brooks film, *As Good as it Gets*, when Simon (Greg Kinear) tells Melvin (Jack Nicholson), "One of the things you have going for you is your willingness to be humiliated." It helps me remember that I chose this struggle, and that it's simply part of the territory of learning anything new. Perhaps all of us who humble ourselves take some solace from the fact that "God opposes the proud, but gives grace to the humble."[109] It helps us understand the importance of God's grace.

Are we being led or called to become unimportant?

When I returned to horseback riding some years ago, I wondered if there was a calling inherent in this activity. I wondered if I would feel God's leading in what seemed to be merely fun, although I approached it with some of the same zeal and determination that I brought to my own work. After some experimentation with various competitions, I decided to take up reining, which is considered the most difficult form of Western riding, much like dressage is considered the most difficult form of English riding because of the subtlety involved and the difficult maneuvers that both horse and rider need to learn. As I write this book, I've now been working at this for three years, taking lessons a few times a week and working with the excellent trainer mentioned in Chapter 2, Danie Ray Hewlett. I'm a rookie, but not just any rookie. For those of us who are truly new at this, we're called "the green rookie" and sometimes "the green-as-grass rookie". There are a lot of us in any horse show, and sometimes it's even a bit painful to watch us ride.

I found great joy in this activity, and great frustration. I wasn't aiming to become the best there was, since I knew that was impossible. I simply wanted to be OK and to experience the joy of riding. But I often wondered if God was leading me, or moving me, in this activity, and if there was something spiritual I was supposed to learn and whether this activity could help develop my spirituality further and whether it had any relationship to my career.

As time went on, I began to learn a number of lessons. I learned to put the focus on the process of learning, not on the goal, since the goal seemed so difficult to achieve. I learned to remember joy when I got frustrated. I learned to care about my horse, and when I sold one horse, to take my responsibility very seriously of making sure the horse had a good owner. A Christian

270

friend reminded me that "compassion for animals is counted as righteousness."[110]

I also began to believe that one of the most important attributes that we bring to anything we do is not always our mastery, but our attitude. When I started to compete, I noticed that people I didn't know began to comment on my riding. They didn't talk about how well I rode (I didn't), or about how pretty my horse is (which he is!), but they commented on my smile. Sometimes five or ten or even more people would come up after I rode and told me that clearly I was enjoying what I was doing, or mentioned how joyful or happy I seemed to be, or what a nice smile I had. More than once, the judge announced, at the end of my time in the show ring, that if there was an award for smiling, I would get first place. A friend of mine sitting in the audience said she heard people around her say, "That woman reminds us what it's all about – having fun! We too often forget the reason we do this!"

We usually do these activities because they bring us joy, but along the way, we can miss the point and begin to think of them as work, just as we can miss the point in our work and forget the joy. Joy and gladness are harbingers of the Holy Spirit. We begin to find the joy in a new activity that we originally felt when we began our work. By entering in, once again, to an activity that we do for the pure joy of it, we often refind the joy in the work we've mastered. We remember, once again, what it's supposed to be about.

The faith we have in the results really needs to be faith that God will use our gifts in unpredictable ways. Perhaps the real gift in these areas where we aren't masters isn't winning, or achieving something earth-shattering or heaven-making, but smiling, contributing, kindness, grace, care, and expressing joy and gladness. We always have the possibility of brightening up the world.

This should be true in anything we do. There are many who work in jobs that will never bring them any kind of notice. It might even be work that demands little skill, and many might wonder what good the job is doing. But what they bring to the job might be their good humor, their helpfulness, their kindness, their grace. No matter what we do, we can help manifest the Kingdom which is among us in all situations, just waiting to be expressed.

Choosing to be unimportant again may actually keep us from an unwanted fall from grace that can come to those who become too puffed up.

Our fear of the fall

There are many characters in the Bible who experienced a mighty fall. Most didn't choose to become unimportant. They were forced into it. Just when everything seemed harmonious and good, Adam and Eve were exiled from their lovely life. Joseph's fortunes rose and fell and rose and fell and rose again. Jesus had times of great adulation from the crowds, and other times when few stood by his side. Even the great kings, such as Saul, David, and Solomon, fell from their mighty thrones. "Oh, how the mighty have fallen!" says David in 2 Samuel.[111]

The mighty becoming unimportant through no desire of their own can be found in many stories and newspaper accounts such as the reversal of fortunes of Leona Helmsley, Martha Stewart, Jim and Tammy Faye

Bakker, Ken Lay, Ted Haggard, and Sandi Patti. Some believed they were doing God's work but got off track. Some got off track because what comes around goes around, and sometimes comes right back at those who harm others.

We have enough examples to feel the precariousness of any success. Those who are spiritual might wonder why God would help build up their work, only to tear it down. If we know the fragility of riches and prosperity and fame, then we also recognize that these fragile structures can fall at any time. We might go through our lives wondering if God will pull the rug from beneath us at any moment. We can easily become fearful about our success, and about God's arbitrary decisions about our lives.

Yet, if we're doing God's work, why would everything we had worked for disintegrate? Would God really want to do this to us? Why do some, spiritual or not, sustain their success for the rest of their lives, and others become unimportant again?

The rise and fall of the veggies

Phil Vischer has some insights into why the mighty fall and can sometimes rise again. Phil is the creator of *Veggie Tales*, children's animated films that use vegetables as characters to communicate moral lessons and Biblical ideas, or as Phil describes them: "*Veggie Tales* is a series of children's videos where limbless talking vegetables act out Bible stories." It became one of the best-selling video series of any kind, selling more than 40 million videos and outselling even Barney, Scooby-Doo and Pokemon.

Phil was labeled as one of the ten people to watch in religion worldwide, and written up in *People Magazine*, *Time* and *Newsweek*. It was, by any account, a story of a dream come true and a great success story.

Phil began *Veggie Tales* in 1993. Before long, they had sold over 10 million videos. Fans wrote them letters. Their company began producing books, records, computer games, toys, a feature film. Phil began to compare himself to Walt Disney. By 2000 he had over 200 people working for him.

But just as *Veggie Tales* reached the pinnacle of success, things began to go wrong. People at the company couldn't get along with each other. Sales stopped growing. The company began to lay people off. A feature film they produced didn't do well. And as everything began to fall apart, Phil kept thinking, "OK God, I think maybe I can still work this out somehow – still keep this going – if you'll just help." Phil prayed for God's help and realized God could have helped. But he didn't. The company went bankrupt, and Phil could do nothing but watch it disintegrate.

During this time, Phil received a letter. "I got an email from a woman I have never met, whom I don't believe had ever met me. She thanked me for the work I was doing and talked about the impact it was having and then she closed by warning me to keep an eye on my pride. For about a year the emails came." And the emails kept saying the same thing, "warning me to keep an eye on my pride."

Then a very godly woman Phil knew told him something: "I don't think this crisis is about God and *Veggie Tales*," she said. "I think this is about God and Phil."

As Phil watched his dream dissolve into bankruptcy,

he began to get the lesson: "If God gives you a dream, and breathes life into it, and shows up in it, and it dies, it may be that God wants you to know what's more important: the dream or him. And you may get back your dream, or you may not, and you may live the rest of your life without it. But that will be OK, because you'll have God."

Why does it become important to let go of our dreams? "Because anything you are unwilling to let go of is an idol, and you are in sin."

When Phil realized this, he began to wait upon the Lord. He began to read the Bible, pray, and to experience a sense of "giving up" and "dying". And shortly after, ideas began to come again. He began to build again, but with God in the center and without the same concerns about doing everything and being important and achieving and achieving some more.

Phil learned the lesson of the Fall. Of course, many do not. Some stay fallen. But some get reborn and begin again.

Grounding ourselves

Missionary Lisa Borden also sees that the Fall comes from pride: "Regardless of our field, as we succeed we need to hold on hard to the truth that we are not superstars, superheroes or even just a step above the people around us. We are those who have been given the opportunity to succeed and that opportunity doesn't mean we are more worthy as human beings. Who we are and how we behave along the way of our success matters. An enormously wealthy donor may think he is indispensable to the work of an organization, but he is not. Likewise, a gifted volunteer or long-term staff person can just as easily begin to believe that 'the work' can't succeed without them. It is healthy to purposefully take ourselves out of the circles where we are recognized and applauded and just get grounded again in the reality that all are created equal. The choice to hold onto the knowledge of our humanity, not disdainfully but with a joyous embrace, assists us in avoiding a self-importance that will ultimately do more damage than the good our great skill-set can achieve."

Giving out of our unimportance

As we do good and do well in our work, we may see our contributions as coming from our mastery and our individuality. But our success also opens up to us the possibility of giving out of our anonymity, and giving to those who don't know who we are and how important we truly are. It allows us to recognize how very much we have to give – in attitudes, skills and money. It also helps us recognize how complex we are as God's people. In the vocabulary of film and theater, we would be called multidimensional characters. There is far more to us than meets the eye. As the poet Gerard Manley Hopkins says, "The world is charged with the grandeur of God!" And so are we. As the Holy Spirit inhabits us, it builds up its power within us and yearns to reach outward to others. In most cases, our charity and love is given to those who know nothing about us, but are mightily thankful for our compassion. Out of this relationship of giving, we can also find mutuality with others and discover a connection not through our greatness, but through the small things in life.

Alex Lo is a business owner from Singapore who distributes software and has done well in his work. He says, "I am free from having to worry about where the next meal is coming from or whether the bank will remove the roof over my head or whether my car will be repossessed. This freedom allows me to think more about his Kingdom and his subjects. As a contented business owner, the freedom of time allows me to serve in various capacities in church and para-church organizations. Besides my active involvement as a deacon and member of the executive committee at my church, I am also serving with the Christian Business Man's Committee (CBMC) and Navigators. I am also blessed to be able to serve as a member of my church mission board and still actively go out regularly for missions in South-East Asia where we minister to the indigenous people there."

Alex has found plenty of opportunities to express the love of the Holy Spirit. "I realize that a lot more can be done for the education of the indigenous people in South-East Asia, as most of them live in secluded places and may not be able to afford studying in the local universities. It is very challenging for them to own a PC when there isn't electricity at their doorstop. Hence I am starting a scholarship program to sponsor their brightest to give them an opportunity to pursue higher education. Can you imagine two persons' scholarships for four years being taken care of for the price of a business-class ticket to the US?"

He found other places for outreach. "In June this year, I was privileged to be able to travel with a few doctors to do some health screening, and you might have already guessed some of the common ailments would be due to the absence of piped water, which we take for granted here. They suffer many skin ailments and malnutrition as a result. Hence we are praying about some water projects, and all these cost something. The frequent trips there have given me a desire to start a simple 'free clinic' with a traveling doctor who can attend to the many who require such aid."

It is often as we encounter those who are considered the lowliest among us, that we recognize our rightful place in the greater scheme of things. We are important enough to have something to give, but we also see the equality of giving and the equality of receiving. Those we give to, also give back to us. We become givers and responders and see that ultimately any work we do is not about how important we are. It's about God.

The fear that we may feel

When we become involved in any kind of giving – whether through our work or through charities – there is often the fear and trepidation of moving into new experiences and new worlds. Many who get involved by expanding their own work into charity work may find that they will be interacting with people and places unlike themselves. It won't be just a matter of making out a check, but of truly becoming involved. Through that involvement, they will encounter the Other, who will stop being a vague, abstract poor and needy person who exists somewhere "out there" and will become "Us", recognizing that there are no boundaries and that the issue of important or not important is no longer relevant.

In the early 1990s, I realized that I was very uninvolved with people unlike myself and that if I were to grow as a Christian, I needed to develop my involvement with social-justice issues. I decided to return to graduate school, and to get an MA in Feminist Theology from Immaculate Heart College Center in Los Angeles. I chose the school partly because the program included forty to eighty hours of work with women in an oppressed situation, and it included study of the experiences of women from non-white, non-First World contexts.

I decided to do my internship in the Philippines, working with WODEEF – the charity mentioned in Chapter 7 which works with indigenous people on the islands of Cebu and Mindanao and focuses on education, micro-lending, and sustainable agriculture.

As I was flying to the Philippines with a Business Class upgrade which made me feel amused and ashamed at the same time, I felt great fear and trepidation. I remembered the words said at my seminary graduation by Dr. Davie Napier: "You know you're on the way to the Promised Land by the fear that you feel when you take the first step." I had no idea how I, a middle-class, middle-aged white woman, would do among people so unlike myself.

In the process of spending ten days with the people of WODEEF, I recognized that "There is no Other, there is only Us." The grace, warmth, accessibility, and artistry of the women of WODEEF as they danced and sang to welcome me, the charm of their children, and their authenticity spoke to me much about true connections with others. We weren't all that different. I identified with their small businesses. I understood many of their struggles, which were made far greater than mine by their poverty and the oppression they suffered from many different sources. I understood their yearning for education, for themselves and for their children. I saw how little it takes to make a huge difference in people's lives. And I discovered that I could be a much bigger person than I was, and make far greater contributions than I thought possible.

The success of my work had expanded my possibilities. The money earned, the people I met, the clout I had achieved through my career, had the potential to ripple outward to other people and other lands. The education that taught me how to think through problems in my work could be used to think through other problems.

During my time there, Sister Luz and I talked about education, and how to help more children get through high school and college. Ten years after that trip, the college graduates have grown from one student to twenty-three.

Sister Luz and I talked about farming and what could be done to develop the ability of the indigenous people of that area to grow crops, learn sustainable agriculture, create new income sources, and become more independent and empowered. I liked Sister Luz's idea of buying land to create a farm and a learning center and was surprised when she asked me to buy them the farm. I had no idea about how to do that, until God reminded me (through that still, small, nudging voice) that I had the money for this and it would be used well. Ten years later, the nine-acre farm has grown from land with only five trees and a pond to over thirty varieties of trees, a pond with fish, rice paddies, goats and pigs and chickens, and a farm that is producing income, more each year.

We are put on this earth partly to help people and things grow. We prepare the soil, we plant our seeds, we hope we are in tune with the Holy Spirit and that the Light comes to nurture our work.

We never stop being called. The need to listen remains. Our desire to be in relationship with God and God's desire to be in relationship with us is always present. The work we do is a sacred trust and a blessed opportunity to build up the Kingdom of God and to embrace and expand the work of the Holy Spirit.

Questions for reflection and discussion

1. Have you ever felt you had become too important? What happened?
2. Did you have to learn to become less important? How did you learn this? What satisfaction have you derived through becoming unimportant?
3. What are the many ways that you, or others, give to those who don't care who you are, but who do, nevertheless, need your help? What have you learned from this kind of giving?
4. Have you, or someone you know, had a fall from grace like Phil Vischer? What was the problem that led to the fall?
5. Think about, and/or discuss, the many qualities that you bring to anything you do. How are you able to give through your God-given goodness and through the work of the Holy Spirit within you?

Scripture to consider

Read some of the Scripture about pride and humility: Proverbs 16:19; Luke 14:11; James 4:6; 1 Peter 5:6.

BIBLIOGRAPHY

Ford, Desmond, *How to Survive Personal Tragedy*, Auburn, CA: Good News Unlimited, 1984.

O'Donohue, John, *To Bless the Space Between Us: A Book of Blessings*, New York: Doubleday, 2008.

Palmer, Parker, *The Active Life: A Spirituality of Work, Creativity, and Caring*, San Francisco: Jossey-Bass, 1999.

Wilson, Lloyd Lee, *Essays on the Quaker Vision of Gospel Order*, Philadelphia: Quaker Press, 1996.

Westermann, Claus, *Blessing in the Bible and the Life of the Church*, translated by Keith Crim, Philadelphia: Fortress Press, 1978.

ENDNOTES

1   Isaiah 66:13; Matthew 23:37.

2   *Daily Readings: From Quaker Writings, Ancient & Modern,* edited by Linda Hill Renfer, Serenity Press, Grants Pass, Oregon, copyright 1988, (1990, 1992 – 3rd printing), p. 306, Renfer.

3   I interviewed Loretta Young for my book *When Women Call the Shots* in 1995 and spent about two hours with her.

4   Acts 9:4–6.

5   1 Samuel 3.

6   Beliefnet, http://www.beliefnet.com/story/227/story_22778_1.html

7   http://www.adherents.com/people/pw/Denzel_Washington.html

8   Lloyd Lee Wilson, *Essays on the Quaker Vision of Gospel Order,* Philadelphia: Quaker Press, 1996, p. 121.

9   Wilson, p. 185.

10   Wilson, p. 186.

11   Galatians 5:22–24.

12   Galatians 5:16–21.

13   1 Corinthians 12.

14   Romans 12.

15   Wilson, p. 94.

16   Wilson, p. 83.

17   Wilson, p. 87.

18   Wilson, p. 184. Lloyd Lee Wilson gives a more extensive and insightful analysis of Jonah and Isaiah in his book *Essays on the Quaker Vision of Gospel Order.*

19   "Millie" words and music by Joni Harms and Wood Newton, Rodeo and Radio (BMI/EMI Blackwood Music, 2001 from CD, "After All")

20   1 Chronicles 4.

21   Luke 12:48.

22   Søren Kierkegaard, from *The Humor of Kierkegaard: An Anthology*, edited and introduced by Thomas C. Oden, Princeton University Press, 2004, p. 50.

23   Søren Kierkegaard, *The Concluding Unscientific Postscript*, translated by David F. Swenson and Walter Lowrie, Princeton University Press, 1941, p. 94.

24   Kierkegaard, *The Concluding Unscientific Postscript*, p. 327.

25   From the Apostles' Creed.

26   Billy Graham, *Just as I Am: The Autobiography of Billy Graham*, New York: HarperOne/Zondervan, 1997, 10th Anniversary Edition, p. 130.

27   Graham, p. 138.

28   Graham, p. 136.

29   Graham, p. 139.

30   Graham, pp. 135–40.

31   From David Van Biema, "Mother Theresa's Crisis of Faith", *Time Magazine*, August 23, 2007. Also mentioned in a number of other articles.

32   Quoted on many different websites.

33   This quotation appears on many websites, but none give a specific source.

34   Hebrews 11.

35   James 2:26.

36   Pierre Teilhard de Chardin, *Hymn of the Universe*, Harper & Row, New York: 1961, p. 134.

37   Teilhard de Chardin, pp. 83–4.

38   C. S. Lewis, *Mere Christianity*, New York: Macmillan 1952, p. 117.

39   Matthew 12:43–45.

40   From "We plow the fields and scatter", 1782, translated by Jane M. Campbell.

41   Deuteronomy 33:13.

42   Genesis 39:5; 2 Samuel 7:29.

43   Psalm 28:9.

44   Psalm 65:10.

45   Deuteronomy 28.

46   Job 42.

47   Psalm 29:11.

48   Matthew 7:9.

49   Matthew 6:33.

50   Jonathan Edwards, 1703-1758.

51   Quoted in Matthew Fox, *Original Blessing*, New York: Tarcher/Putnam, 2000, p. 43. I am indebted to Fox for his development of this insight.

52   Fox, p. 5.

53   Fox, p. 44.

54   Fox, p. 53.

55   Fox, p. 113.

56   Zechariah 9:17 (NJB).

57   Deuteronomy 28:8, 12 (NJB).

58   1 Peter 3:10–12 (NJB).

59   Psalm 104:34 (NJB).

60   Claus Westermann, *Blessing in the Bible and the Life of the Church*, translated by Keith Crim, Philadelphia: Fortress Press, 1978, p. 13.

61   Westermann, p. 19.

62   Westermann, pp. 18–19.

63   Westermann, p. 67.

64   Westermann, p. 85.

65   John O'Donohue, *To Bless the Space Between Us: A Book of Blessings*, New York: Doubleday, 2008, p. 207.

66   O'Donohue, p. 205.

67   O'Donohue, pp. 198–199.

68   Westermann, p. 43.

69   This actually is not a biblical verse, although it's often attributed to the Bible. It is based on verses such as John 15:19; 17:14; James 1:27; 4:4; 1 John 2:15.

70   Galatians 5.

71   1 Samuel 1:10–11.

72   Philippians 4:12–13.

73   Genesis 1.

74   Genesis 12:3.

75   Numbers 22:6.

76   Luke 6:28.

77   O'Donohue, p. 146.

78   *O – The Oprah Magazine*, January 2008, p. 213.

79   Genesis 39:23 (NJB).

80   Genesis 4:7 (NJB).

81   Exodus 20 (NJB).

82   There are a number of books that discuss Catal Huyuk. Archaeologist James Mellart led the dig there and wrote *Catal Huyuk: A Neolithic Town in Anatolia* by James Mellart, McGraw Hill, New York: 1967. Marija Gimbutas discusses it in *The Language of the Goddess*, San Francisco: Harper SanFrancisco, 1989, and *The Goddesses and Gods of Old Europe: 6500-3500 B.C. Myths and Cult Images*, Berkeley: University of California Press, 1981. Riane Eisler mentions this city in *The Chalice and the Blade: Our History, Our Future*, New York: HarperSanFrancisco, 1995.

83   This is quoted on a number of websites. It was a quotation my mother often told me when I was growing up in Wisconsin.

84   1 Corinthians 12:4–6 (NJB).

85   1 Corinthians 12:15–17 (NJB).

86   From the Scott Bader website (www.scottbader.com) and the *Scott Bader Handbook*.

87   From the article "Scott Bader Company Limited", sent by Sue Carter, Commonwealth Secretary of Bader Company in the U.S.

88   Genesis 3:17–19 (NJB).

89   These sins are mentioned again and again, but you can

find some listed in Proverbs 15, Romans 2, Philippians 2, Colossians 3, 2 Timothy 3, James 3, 1 Peter 2, and 3 John 10.

90   C. S. Lewis, *Mere Christianity*, New York: Macmillan 1952, p. 94-5.

91   Proverbs 27:15 (NJB).

92   Proverbs 17:22; 18:14.

93   Hebrews 12:3.

94   From *Strictly Ballroom*, directed by Baz Luhrmann, written by Craig Pearce, Baz Luhrmann, and Andrew Bovell.

95   1 Thessalonians 5:17.

96   From Beliefnet – http://www.beliefnet.com/story/133/story-13350-1.html

97   Philippians 3:10 (NJB).

98   Parker J. Palmer, *The Active Life: A Spirituality of Work, Creativity, and Caring*, San Francisco: Jossey-Bass, 1999, p. 7.

99   Palmer, p. 11.

100   Palmer, p. 17.

101   Palmer, p. 17.

102   Palmer, p. 23.

103   Palmer, p. 27.

104   Palmer, p. 24.

105   Denys the Areopagite (fifth/sixth century AD), also known as Pseudo-Dionysius or Pseudo-Denys.

106   Speaking of God from all creation is known as cataphatic theology. Being reduced to silence is known as apophatic theology.

107   Desmond Ford, *How to Survive Personal Tragedy*, Auburn, CA: Good News Unlimited, 1984, p. 60.

108   Ford, p. 81.

109   James 4:6.

110   A paraphrase of Proverbs 12:10.

111   2 Samuel 1:19, 25, 27.